KAREN EHMAN

WHAT MATTERS MOST

A STUDY OF PHILIPPIANS

LifeWay Press® Nashville, Tennessee

Published by LifeWay Press® • ©2018 Karen Ehman
Reprinted September 2018

ISBN 978-1-4158-6692-4
Item 005189426
Dewey decimal classification: 227.6
Subject heading: BIBLE. N.T. PHILIPPIANS--STUDY AND TEACHING \ WOMEN \ CHRISTIAN LIFE

To order additional copies of this resource, write LifeWay Church Resources Customer Service; One LifeWay Plaza; Nashville, TN 37234; fax order to 615.251.5933; call toll-free 800.458.2772; email orderentry@lifeway.com; order online at www.lifeway.com; or visit the LifeWay Christian Store serving you.

Printed in the United States of America

Adult Ministry Publishing, LifeWay Church Resources,
One LifeWay Plaza, Nashville, TN 37234

TABLE OF CONTENTS

4 **ABOUT THE AUTHOR**

5 **INTRODUCTION**

6 **WEEK 1:** *The Gospel*

28 **WEEK 2:** *Heavenly Minded & Earthly Good*

52 **WEEK 3:** *Living for Christ & Others*

78 **WEEK 4:** *How & Why We Run the Race*

108 **WEEK 5:** *Turning Worry into Worship*

134 **WEEK 6:** *Chasing Contentment*

164 **WEEK 7:** *Partnership in the Gospel*

168 **LEADER GUIDE**

171 **ENDNOTES**

ABOUT THE AUTHOR

Karen Ehman has possessed a love of studying God's Word since the age of sixteen. She began reading a Bible given to her by the across-the-street country church in rural Michigan where she first heard and responded to the gospel at a youth group event. From there, she graduated from Spring Arbor University, began teaching Bible studies in her home church, and now teaches women at events across the country through her books and Bible studies. She's also involved with online Bible teaching to thousands of women around the world.

Karen is a Proverbs 31 Ministries speaker, a writer for the First 5 Bible study app, and a New York Times best-selling author of twelve books including *Keep It Shut: What to Say, How to Say It, and When to Say Nothing at All*. She has been featured on numerous media outlets including FoxNews.com, Redbook.com, Crosswalk.com, FamilyLife.com, and HomeLife Magazine. Married to her college sweetheart, Todd, and the mother of three, Karen enjoys antique hunting, cheering for the Detroit Tigers, and feeding the many teens and young adults who gather around her kitchen island for a taste of Mama Karen's cooking. Connect with her at karenehman.com or inquire about speaking engagements by visiting proverbs31.org/speakers.

Proverbs 31 Ministries exists to be a trusted friend who will take you by the hand and walk by your side, leading you one step closer to the heart of God through:

Free online daily devotions | First 5 Bible study app | Daily radio program | Books and resources | Online Bible Studies | COMPEL Writers Training: CompelTraining.com

TO LEARN MORE ABOUT PROVERBS 31 MINISTRIES, CALL 877-731-4663 OR VISIT PROVERBS31.ORG.

INTRODUCTION

This world is full of trials, disappointments, temptations, fractured friendships, and financial hardships. Circumstances that threaten to knock the joy right out of us swirl about, sending us into an emotional state of despair. We may regret our past choices, feel pressured in our present situations, or fear what our futures may hold.

When such conditions rattle our souls, where can we go for comfort—to gain a new perspective? We might reach out to a friend for advice. We could pick up our phones to escape reality for a while, diving into the picture-perfect world of social media. We might go for a walk to clear our heads or even flop ourselves on our beds for a nap, hoping we'll wake up with a fresh slate, ready to start all over again.

But none of these options offer a permanent solution. They are only temporary, mind-numbing fixes that soon fizzle, leaving us still wallowing in weariness. There has to be a better way.

And there is. We find it when we flip our Bibles open and make our way to the New Testament Book of Philippians, determined to deeply drink in its life-changing truths about *what matters most.*

This short letter—only one hundred and four verses—makes the audacious claim that despite the difficulties we might face, we can experience true contentment and live in real joy. Paul wrote this letter while a prisoner—most likely in the city of Rome. In fact, he was possibly facing execution for his faith. However, no book in the entire Bible is so filled with deep joy and soul-settled contentment as the letter to the Philippians.

While few of us are in a physical prison, we are, in effect, held prisoner nonetheless by many of the topics touched upon in this book. We feel enslaved to the opinions of others, especially our critics. We are shackled by the chains of comparison that prevent us from experiencing true contentment. Our thought lives are a tangled mass of regret, doubt, worry, and sinful thoughts. Thankfully, Philippians holds the key that will unlock the secret of contentment as we apply the truths taught on its pages.

Okay, go grab a cup of something delicious, and let's plunge into Philippians, discovering the truth about *what matters most.*

Cheering you on in your walk with the Lord,

Karen

WEEK 1
WHAT MATTERS MOST
THE GOSPEL

Now I want you to know, brothers and sisters, that what has happened to me has actually advanced the gospel.

PHILIPPIANS 1:12

VIEWER GUIDE

FAVORITE QUOTES

STAND-OUT SCRIPTURES

Video teaching sessions available for purchase at *LifeWay.com/WhatMattersMost*

GROUP GUIDE

ICEBREAKER

Have you ever become the person you used to make fun of (like what happened with Karen and the bird lady)? Or is there an aspect of your life now that you were certain years ago would never be said of you? Share your thoughts with the group.

1. *Which of the two categories of topics that will pop up most often in the Letter of Philippians—relationships and circumstances—do you most need a biblical perspective on? Why?*

2. *What aspect of the city of Philippi or the beginning of the church there did you most enjoy learning about?*

3. *In what ways does the "fly over verse" Philippians 1:1 take on a new meaning for you now?*

4. *The church at Philippi was made up of people who were culturally, ethnically, and economically diverse. What are some practical ways you can reach out and get to know other Christians who do not look like you or live like you?*

5. *In Philippians 1:3-5, Paul stated he was grateful for his fellow Christians' "partnership in the gospel." The original language has financial undertones, implying they used their money and resources to care for each other. When have you financially helped care for another believer or were the recipient of such help? How is this being a partner in the gospel? How does it reflect the salvation story?*

6. *Paul said that his imprisonment had actually caused the gospel to advance (Phil. 1:12-14). We may not be in a physical prison, but some situations we face might feel like a prison—financial hardship, divorce, wayward children, sickness, or other difficulties. Have you ever seen such a prison—whether in your own life or in the life of another—actually serve as an avenue to advance the gospel? Explain.*

ON YOUR OWN

Are you currently facing a situation where you are tempted to cry, *Lord, get me out of here*? How might the script flip if instead you asked, *Father, why have You brought me here*? Take a few moments to write out a brief prayer about this situation and the attitude adjustment you long for.

PRAYER TIME

End your time together by taking prayer requests related to the topics in this week's session. Call on one person to pray for your group. May God grow your faith as you begin this study of *What Matters Most*.

INTRODUCTION

I'm somewhat of an old soul. Although I love to keep up with what is happening in culture and try to understand the latest technology, there is something about all things old-fashioned that I crave and adore. An antique farm table. An old market basket sitting on that old farm table. And to top it off? A nearly one hundred-year-old book nestled in the basket ready to be read by a curious mind longing to slow down, lean in, and learn from its ancient words.

I collect such timeworn books (along with some of the period furniture and retro baskets too). One day while curled up on the sofa with such a book, a section of typeset letters leapt off the page at me. I'd just wiped the dust from the olive green cloth board cover of this volume—an exposition on the Book of Philippians written by a pastor and professor at Princeton. When I carefully turned the yellowing pages to the foreword, my eyes fell on this poetic passage:

PAUL'S LETTER TO THE CHURCH AT PHILIPPI

"Here is a 'hymn of joy.' At least the composition is pitched to that high key. The music is the more appealing because its accompaniment sounds the notes of privation and loneliness and poverty and pain.

The lines are penned by a prisoner. They are designed to express his gratitude to the friends whose gift has brought relief. More fully do they reveal his conscious relationship to a divine Lord.

The service of Christ is the very sphere of his life;

the spirit of Christ is the temper of his mind;

the perfection of Christ is the goal of his effort;

the power of Christ is the secret of his triumph.

His artless unfolding of personal experience points every reader to the one pathway of peace and strength and unfailing gladness.

Here one can learn to sing songs in the night." —**Pastor Charles R. Erdman**[1]

How I love the picture painted in those words!

Here one can learn to sing songs in the night.

Paul, the imprisoned author of this letter to the infant church at Philippi, had many reasons to despair. He wrote of having been deserted by most of his friends. Others—even fellow Christian leaders—had spoken out against him, hoping to get him into trouble with the ruling government. In fact, Paul was possibly facing execution for his faith. However, no book in the Bible is so filled with deep joy as the Book of Philippians.

What was Paul's secret? How in the world—literally in this human world in which our bodies dwell—could he find the strength not only to be content with his circumstances, but to fix his thoughts on heaven and walk in authentic joy? How could he learn to sing songs in the night?

This letter, written not one hundred years ago but almost two thousand years ago, contains the mysterious musical score that will enable us today to sing such songs in the night. We'll be able to belt out these melodies as we discover what Paul's words and life fleshed out: When we understand what matters most, we can experience joy no matter what.

Are you ready? Snuggle up in your own special spot—whether a nostalgic couch, a trendy table at a coffee house, an office cubicle, or a rustic bench in the park. Together let's learn *what matters most.*

READ IT CAREFULLY

This week we will focus on Philippians 1:1-19. Begin by reading these verses through in one sitting or at least over the course of one day. Once you have finished, go back and read them again slowly. As you do, note the verses that jump out at you and why. Do you have a question about a particular verse or portion of Scripture? Does the section encourage you as you face a current situation? Does it convict or challenge you? Record the verses that stand out as well as your reasons for choosing them in the space provided.

VERSE/VERSES	REASON IT STANDS OUT

Now, go back and place a star beside the verse that most encouraged or challenged you in the text. Then put a question mark beside the one that most puzzled you.

The Book of Philippians covers many topics. Let's keep a running list of these matters as we read through the text each week. In the space that follows, jot down any topics covered in the first nineteen verses of chapter one along with the corresponding verse(s) where you found the topic. To help get you started, I've already noted a few.

TOPIC	VERSE WHERE IT IS FOUND
Thankfulness for Christian friends	*Verse 3*
Joyful prayer for believing friends	*Verse 4*
Confidence in Christ's continuing good work in us	*Verse 5-6*

Now that you have read these verses carefully,
answer the following questions:

Did you discover anything new in this passage you had not noticed in the Bible before? If so, record it here.

Did you spy an old familiar verse in this passage anywhere?
If so, which one?

Did you notice any interesting topic covered in this passage you didn't know the Bible covered? If so, what topic?

Great job! Now, spend a moment or two praying that God will help your mind to dwell on these verses over the next week. Also pray that He will enlighten your study as we dive deeper into these verses in the next section.

STUDY IT PRAYERFULLY

In the last section, you carefully read this week's passage, took note of any verses that specifically challenged or puzzled you, and jotted down the different topics covered in this first chunk of the letter to the Philippians. Time now to drill down a little deeper.

ON SERVANTS AND SAINTS

In the first verse of chapter one, how are Paul and Timothy described?

The original Greek word that is translated in our English Bibles as "servant," "bond servant," or "slave" is the word *doulos*. In Paul's day, there were three ways a person could become a *doulos* or slave/servant. They could be born slaves. Any child whose birth parents were slaves was automatically deemed a slave as well. Secondly, a person could become a slave by conquest when—in a war between two countries or tribes—the victorious army captured the people of the defeated side and forced them into involuntary servanthood. And finally, a person could become a slave due to debt. People in poverty sometimes sold themselves or their offspring into slavery in order to pay off a debt they had incurred.

Paul describes himself and his companion Timothy as "servants of Christ." We must not skip over this verse without thinking about the importance we might unearth from it.

An old song from my teenage years by musician Bob Dylan argues that in life you are going to have to serve somebody. "Well, it may be the devil or it may be the Lord, but you're gonna have to serve somebody."[2] And you know what? This notion isn't just a catchy, classic rock tune. It is a rock-solid, scriptural truth.

We are born sinners. Sin rules over us. Sin conquers us. We can easily see parallels between our being slaves to sin and slavery in biblical times. There were a few ways that slaves could be released from bondage. They could purchase their freedom for a price, if they possessed enough money. Or if they didn't have the money, their freedom could be granted if someone else was able to pay the cost required for their redemption. Or they could earn their freedom by working off their debt over a set period of time, usually several years. And of course, death brought an end to their slavery when they passed from this life into the next.

In contrast, our slavery to sin can only be remedied one way: through Jesus. He is the One who purchased our freedom through His sacrificial death, guaranteeing that we could be freed from the bondage of sin once and for all. We cannot earn our salvation. Jesus already earned it for us and offers it to us freely.

Paul showcases this powerful truth, which affects how you read verse 1. We are no longer slaves to sin. We are servants of Christ.

Also in verse 1, Paul refers to all the believers in Philippi by what word?

When we think of the word *saint*, a particularly holy person from the past might pop into our minds. But the Greek word for *saint* does not mean a perfectly-behaved person who never sins. It refers to someone who has been consecrated or set apart. That's us. As Christians, we have been set apart by God through Christ in order to carry out the work of the church here on earth. We are chosen, "a royal priesthood, a holy nation," a people belonging to God (1 Pet. 2:9). Another rendition of this word means *different*. Christians are supposed to be different from the rest of the world.

When you think of our current culture, in what ways are we supposed to be different or set apart from others who do not claim to know Christ? List specific ways of thinking or behaving. Be sure these aren't just your opinions of certain activities or behaviors but are actually tethered to what we read in the Bible.

Are any of these particularly difficult for you to do? If so, why? Write a prayer asking God to help you to be set apart and different in your thinking and actions.

INCLUSIVE GREETING

Writing handwritten letters is an art that has all but fallen by the wayside. Today we type out emails, tap out texts, or send people private messages on social media. Usually, we dive right into the subject matter at hand. But the old-fashioned letter was a communication tool that began with a heartfelt and heartwarming greeting. (I can still remember having to write out various possible "salutations" to begin a friendly letter in my 7th grade English class.)

The letter to the Philippians starts in this way. In verse 2, Paul uses two specific, heartwarming words in his greeting. Fill them in below.

______________ to you and ____________ from God our Father and the Lord Jesus Christ.

Look up the words *grace* and *peace* in a dictionary, and write out their definitions below.

Grace:

Peace:

In the culture of Paul's day, *grace* was usually used in a greeting to Gentiles. The Greek word for *grace* is *charis*. It means joy, pleasure, beauty, and brightness. It is even connected to our English word *charm*. The beauty of grace in Christ is that we are born into a relationship with our loving Father. It is not earned. It is a gift. And because of this gift we are no longer under the law but under His loving grace.

Peace on the other hand was used when addressing a Jewish audience. The original word is *eirēnē*. This type of peace isn't just one that is void of trouble. It means complete and total well-being.

It is interesting that Paul uses both of these common words of salutation—one meant for Greeks, one meant for Jews—in the opening of his communication to the Philippian church. This church was made up of both types of people. We're given some insight into the church membership in Acts 16. It was thought that there was no synagogue in the city, so Jews met together down at the river's shore to worship. In the Book of Acts, we see Paul speaking with Lydia, "a dealer in purple cloth" and convert to Judaism who was at the river (Acts 16:14). The origin of the church of Philippi can be traced to his meeting with her that day as she responded to the gospel and was baptized along with the members of her household. Paul and his companions then stayed with her for a time.

Following Paul's encounter with Lydia, he cast a demon out of a slave girl. This resulted in Paul's and Silas's imprisonment, which led to the salvation of the Philippian jailer and his family (Acts 16:16-34). These three key people—Lydia, the slave girl, and the prison guard—were quite possibly the first converts in the city of Philippi, and they couldn't be more different! Lydia was a wealthy woman from Asia. The slave girl was poverty-stricken and Greek. The jailer was a middle-class Philippian. This shows us that the gospel is for everyone.

Additionally, the city of Philippi was full of non-Jews; thus the church would also have many such people in its congregation. There were populations of both Greeks and Romans and, although Latin was the official language, most people spoke Greek. By using both the words *grace* and *peace* in his opening greeting, Paul was subtly saying what is overtly said elsewhere in Scripture: "There is no Jew or Greek, slave or free, male and female; since you are all one in Christ Jesus" (Gal. 3:28).

Today, if you were penning a letter to an infant church, think of the different types of people that might be in its ranks. What would be an inclusive greeting you might write to them? Jot it out.

CHRISTIAN CAMARADERIE

Do you have any Christian friends who are more like siblings to you? Because you share a common faith, your friendship runs deep. You have forged a strong bond with them over the years as together you each have grown in your walks with the Lord. Such friends are crucial. Helpful. Encouraging. And usually, lifelong.

In verses 3-7, Paul gives thanks to God for his Christian friends in the church at Philippi. He uses phrases like "partnership in the gospel," "I have you in my heart," and "partners with me in grace." Think about your own close Christian friends for a moment.

In what ways do you feel a partnership with them?

Does the phrase "I have you in my heart" resonate with you when you think about your friends who are believers (v.7)? If so, how?

Just how important is it to have close Christian friends? Look up the following verses, and jot down your thoughts about the truth found in each passage.
Proverbs 11:14

Proverbs 13:20

Ecclesiastes 4:9-10

John 15:12-13

1 Thessalonians 5:11

Is any pleasure on earth as great as a circle of Christian friends by a good fire?

C. S. LEWIS[3]

Think of a close Christian friend. Got that person in mind? Good. Now, using Philippians 1:9-11 as your template, craft a prayer for them. You may even wish to jot them a handwritten note with your prayer to encourage them spiritually and brighten their day.

In verses 12-19, Paul speaks of his imprisonment. He is in physical confinement, held captive. However, he does not allow his chains to shackle him spiritually. Look at these verses again, and then answer the following questions.

How has Paul's imprisonment affected his sharing of the gospel?

How has his boldness affected the boldness of others?

In verses 15-18, what shows that the proclamation of the gospel is the priority to Paul?

Today we may not be in an actual brick and bars prison, but there are many things that seek to hold us captive.

Has something ever gripped you that actually turned out to be beneficial because it enabled you to encourage and strengthen someone's spiritual growth? Explain.

Has a situation or circumstance held you prisoner but God used it to share the gospel with others? Explain.

LIVE IT OUT PRACTICALLY

We've covered many topics through this week's passage. We have explored what it means to be servants of Christ. We've unearthed the real meaning of the word *saint*. We've talked about grace, peace, and true Christian friendship. And most of all, we have explored the concept of how the gospel can be advanced despite our difficult circumstances. It's time now for living out what we have learned.

AN OUTWARD SYMBOL OF AN INWARD ATTITUDE

I don't have a ton of jewelry. Of course, I have a few pieces I treasure, such as my wedding ring, another ring my husband gave me on our twenty-fifth anniversary, and a necklace with all of my children's names engraved on it. I also have the gold watch my mother gave me when I turned twenty-one. And, yes, I still have in my possession my high school class ring, complete with my birthstone in it and my initials on the side.

Beyond that, I only have one other treasured piece of jewelry. It is a simple silver toe ring. Yes. A toe ring. Let me explain.

In the Old Testament, if a slave loved his master and chose to stay with him even after his time of servitude was completed, the master would pierce the slave's ear. This was an outward symbol of loyalty and lifetime commitment to his master (Ex. 21:1-6; Deut. 15:12-17). I decided I wanted something to remind me that I am a servant of Christ and eternally belong to Him. I already had pierced ears, so I needed something else I could feel and see with my own eyes without looking in the mirror. I chose to start wearing a sterling silver toe ring.

I don this piece of jewelry to remind me that I am a slave of Christ. Therefore, my thoughts, words, and actions should be in alignment with His will. There've been times when I started to behave badly or use my words wrongly, such as lashing out in anger at a loved one, but then spied the ring on my left foot (or, in the winter, saw the identical thumb ring I wear instead). It's a stark reminder: I am a servant of Christ. Am I acting like one?

Yes, in reality—legally—I am free. I live in a country where I am allowed to do as I like as long as I don't break the laws of the land. However, my toe ring reminds me of this verse:

> *Live as free people, but do not use your freedom as a cover-up for evil; live as God's slaves.*
> **1 PETER 2:16, NIV**

In our Christian culture, too often we use our freedom as a cover-up for evil. No longer is it common for us to view God with respect, standing in awe of His holiness with a healthy fear (reverence) of Him. We have dumbed down God. Made Him our pal. Our buddy. Our assistant who will fetch us anything we desire—well, as long as we ask politely. Instead of us being servants of Christ, we think He is meant to serve us, to grant our wishes, and make our lives comfortable and difficulty-free.

This backward view of our relationships and roles with God is wrong and evil.

For a proper understanding of our place—and God's—look up the following verses, and record what they say about God (and His ability).

Exodus 15:6

Psalm 66:5-7

Isaiah 26:4

Jeremiah 10:12-13

Zephaniah 3:17

Ephesians 3:20-21

Now, in a brief paragraph, describe who God is and who we are as humans in relation to Him.

How does seeing and recording this perspective change your thoughts about God? Have you ever thought of Him as your servant or your wish-granter? Explain. What changes will you make in your thoughts and language toward and about God now that you better understand the truth about who He is and who we are?

On that topic, review our discussion of slavery during Paul's day (p. 15). How does that explanation help you understand your relationship with Christ?

On a scale of 1 to 10, with 1 being *never* and 10 being *always*, how often would you say you think of yourself as a slave of Jesus?

Never *Always*

1 2 3 4 5 6 7 8 9 10

How would you like to see that number change?

Perhaps you will want to score your own bangle or bracelet to remind you that you belong to Christ!

CHALLENGE OF THE WEEK

If you want even more opportunity to put into practice the truths you've learned in this session, choose to complete one of the following challenges. Be ready to share the results of your challenge with your group.

1. WRITE A LETTER. Write a handwritten letter to a close Christian friend expressing what His or her friendship means to you and how it has helped you in your walk with Christ. Start your letter by quoting Philippians 1:3-6, "I give thanks to my God for every remembrance of you, always praying with joy for all of you in my every prayer, because of your partnership in the gospel from the first day until now. I am sure of this, that he who started a good work in you will carry it on to completion until the day of Christ Jesus." Pop it in the mail, and send it off with a prayer.

2. DIVERSIFY YOUR RELATIONSHIPS. The Philippian church was diverse, containing both Jews and non-Jews, as well as people of different social status. Do all your friends look and live just like you? Think of someone who is of a different race, nationality, or economic level than you. Invite them out for coffee to get to know them better, and share the love of Christ with them.

3. WRITE YOUR TESTIMONY. Paul saw his chains as an opportunity to spread the gospel. Has something happened in your life that has placed you in bondage? Can you see Christ and the gospel even in the midst of this sorrowful or painful circumstance? If so, write your testimony of the way God met you in the situation and how the gospel can help others who struggle with such situations. First Peter 3:15-16a urges us: " … in your hearts regard Christ the Lord as holy, ready at any time to give a defense to anyone who asks you for a reason for the hope that is in you. Yet do this with gentleness and respect … " By having your testimony written out, you'll be ready to give the reason for your hope when someone asks. (Then, pray that they will ask!)

MEMORY VERSE

OPTIONAL MEMORY VERSE

There will be optional memory work provided each week to further internalize the message of the passages we study together. To support you in this endeavor, all six passages are printed in the back of the study guide. Feel free to photocopy those pages on paper or card stock, and then cut the verses out. If you are the crafty sort, you could layer the verses on top of some decorative scrapbooking paper.

Keep them in a convenient location—like your vehicle, purse, or laptop bag. You can practice memorizing them while waiting—in the dentist's office, carpool line, or at the Department of Motor Vehicles. (*You could probably memorize the whole Book of Philippians during your wait there!*) Or, you might decide to post them at your kitchen sink or tape them up on your bathroom mirror where you will see them each day. Laminate them with clear contact paper to prevent them from getting splashed.

You may want to see if someone else in your group would like to come early or stay a few minutes after your group time so the two of you can practice saying the verses out loud to each other.

We'll start out with a sweet and simple verse to remind us that our struggles can be used for God's purposes.

Now I want you to know, brothers and sisters, that what has happened to me has actually advanced the gospel.
PHILIPPIANS 1:12

Now I want you to know, brothers and sisters, that what has happened to me has actually advanced the gospel.

PHILIPPIANS 1:12

WEEK 2

WHAT MATTERS MOST

HEAVENLY MINDED & EARTHLY GOOD

Just one thing:
As citizens of
heaven, live your
life worthy of the
gospel of Christ.
PHILIPPIANS 1:27a

VIEWER GUIDE

FAVORITE QUOTES

STAND-OUT SCRIPTURES

GROUP GUIDE

ICEBREAKER

As a child or teenager, did you ever go away to summer camp or to a relative's house for an extended period of time and struggle with homesickness? Tell the group about your experience.

1. *What was significant to you about the three definitions for the Greek word for* depart—to strike camp, to set sail, *and* to solve a problem? *How does each one capture the death of a Christian?*

2. *Call on someone to read aloud Philippians 1:21-26. When it comes to living on earth or going to be with Christ, which would you honestly say you desire most? Why? How can these verses help you gain an eternal perspective on the time you have remaining here on earth?*

3. *The wordplay in Philippians 1:25 translated "to bide and to abide" means both, "I am here" and "I am here* for you." *Do you have a Christian friend who expresses to you "I am here" and "I am here for you" through his or her words and actions? Explain.*

4. *Why is it sometimes hard to remember that we are first and foremost citizens of heaven? Why is it so important that we do so? How can Philippians 1:27-30 help you to gain a proper perspective?*

5. *Discuss this thought:* "Jesus modeled upside-down living and loving. He granted dignity to people and was kind to them because ... they were people. We must do the same thing. Remember, our witness hinges on our walk." *Does your church treat those outside the church the way Jesus treated outsiders? Explain.*

6. *Evaluate how you and your circle of believers are doing in the following areas:*
   - *Standing firm in one spirit, in one accord*
   - *Contending together for the gospel*
   - *Not being frightened in any way by your opponents*

7. *Choose one person to read Philippians 1:29-30 to the group. How have you seen someone's faith strengthened by experiencing suffering? How did that person's suffering affect the lives of those around them?*

ON YOUR OWN

Is there a situation in your life where you have been glancing and gazing backward—staring at your circumstances rather than fixing your eyes upon God? Spend a few moments crafting a prayer to God about this situation.

PRAYER TIME

End your time together by taking prayer requests related to the topics in this session's study. Then call on one person to pray for your group. See you next time!

INTRODUCTION

My friend Thida is a dual citizen. She was born and raised in Cambodia but relocated to the United States when she married Keith, a resident of Michigan. I had the pleasure of not only attending their wedding reception held here in the States, but later writing a letter of recommendation for her when she applied for U. S. citizenship.

For Thida to become a citizen, she had to read and study, becoming well-versed in American history and the laws of our land. After she passed the entrance exam and the committee reviewed her recommendation letters, she was ready to make it official. Her smile stretched wider than the Golden Gate Bridge when she became a full-fledged American. Even though she is now legally a member of our country, she is also still a natural-born citizen of Cambodia.

Today Thida dwells in a quaint Midwestern town, yet she never forgets that her birthplace is a country halfway around the globe. Although she is living out her days as a wife and mom in America's heartland, she is ever cognizant of her beloved homeland and how much being connected to it means to her.

We as Christians are very much like my friend Thida. Though we dwell here on earth, we should be ever cognizant of the fact that we are also citizens of heaven. What we think and how we act here on earth should reflect this truth. As we discover more of Paul's writing in chapter 1 of Philippians, we will gain insight into how citizens of heaven should behave while still dwelling here on this planet. Are you ready, you dual citizen, you? Let's begin!

READ IT CAREFULLY

Let's continue our trek by reading Philippians 1:20-30. Read through this portion of Scripture in one sitting or at least over the course of one day. Once you have finished, go back and read it again slowly, soaking in the meaning of this passage. As you do, note the verses that jump out at you and why. Is it because you have a question about a particular verse or segment of Scripture? Does the content encourage you as you face a current situation? Does it convict, inspire, or challenge you? Record the verses that stand out as well as your reasons for choosing them in the space provided.

VERSE/VERSES	REASON IT STANDS OUT

Now, go back and place a star beside the verse that most encouraged or challenged you. Then put a question mark beside the one that most puzzled you.

Continue your running list of the topics covered in Philippians. Jot down any subjects mentioned in Philippians 1:20-30 along with the corresponding verse reference.

TOPIC	VERSE WHERE IT IS FOUND

Now that you have read these verses carefully,
answer the following questions:

Did you discover anything new in this passage you had not noticed in the Bible before? If so, record it here.

Did you spy an old familiar verse in this passage anywhere?
If so, which one?

Did you notice any interesting topic covered in this passage you didn't know the Bible covered? If so, what topic?

Good work! Now, spend a little time praying that God will help you internalize this chunk of Scripture and maximize your study of it as we cover it more in-depth.

STUDY IT PRAYERFULLY

Now that you've carefully read the passage, it's time to study it verse-by-verse to unearth the meaning and discover some practical application.

UNASHAMED AND UNAFRAID

Is there any more precise picture of expectation, hope, and excitement than young children ready for bed on Christmas Eve? When I was a child, every Christmas Eve my brother and I—unlike many other evenings—would happily cooperate when taking our bubble baths and donning our plaid flannel pajamas. Then we'd pile into our parents' station wagon and cruise our Midwestern hometown to look at the Christmas lights on display. A family at the back of our neighborhood presented a spectacular display complete with a lighted Santa on the roof climbing in the chimney. The Baker family had vintage stockings for all ten of their children, each with the child's name on it, meticulously hung in their huge picture window. Local businesses also got in on the act with twinkling lights and larger-than-life Christmas characters smiling from atop their buildings.

My parents discovered that this little Christmas lights excursion served two purposes: First, it distracted us from our excitement for a while so that our yuletide yikes could calm down a bit. Additionally, it completely tuckered us out so that we would fall asleep in the back seat of the car. Then they no longer needed to provide an answer to the, "How much longer?" question about Santa's arrival. They only needed to carry us to our beds so that the visions of sugar plums could begin their annual dance as we slumbered, awaiting the celebration of Jesus' birth.

In our study passage this week, Paul described in Philippians 1:20 his "eager expectation and hope." This great anticipation pertained to honoring Christ in his body, whether by life or by death, and living in such a way that he would not be ashamed of anything.

> If someone did not know the meaning of the word *expectation*, how would you explain its definition? You may use a dictionary or online resource to help you.

The particular Greek word that Paul used for *expectation* is an out-of-the-ordinary word. In fact, there is no one else in all of Scripture who ever uses the word. It could be that Paul himself concocted and coined it. It is the word *apokaradokia*. Let's break down this long and awkward-looking term.

In the Greek, *apo* means away from, separate, free from. The word *kara* means the head. *Dokein* means to look or seem. When you crochet them all together, the word *apokaradokia* paints a picture of strained expectancy, anxious longing, or earnest expectation—an intense stare that causes one to look away from every lesser thing and fix their gaze on the only thing of true importance.[1]

The one other time Paul used this exact word was in Romans 8:19. There he applied the term directly to the anticipation of each believer receiving a unique, glorified body at Christ's return. This intense longing goes far beyond our childlike excitement each Christmas Eve as we anticipate the celebration of Christ's birth. It is riveted on the future glorious event of the Lord Jesus Christ's return. In our text for this week's study, Paul expressed the hope that he would never be ashamed of the gospel but would courageously honor Christ in his body, in life, and even in death.

How would you describe your excitement about serving Christ and sharing the gospel? Think of a one word answer. Bursting? Passionate? Mild? Lukewarm? Passive?

When you think of conducting yourself in a way that honors God, are you energized by the opportunity to serve or discouraged because you're afraid you'll never measure up? Explain.

The word rendered *hope* in verse 20 is the Greek word *elpis*. It means not just wishful thinking, but hoping with trust and in confidence, certain that the situation will come to pass. Paul's certainty that what he was eagerly expecting would come to pass led to the second half of verse 20: "I will not be ashamed about anything, but that now as always, with all courage, Christ will be highly honored in my body, whether by life or by death."

The apostle Paul was unashamed and unafraid. His identity and purpose were rooted firmly in the gospel of Christ. Therefore, he could live in such a manner that courageously honored Christ in his body, whether he lived or died.

On a scale of 1 to 10, with 1 being *extremely timid and reluctant* and 10 being *completely unashamed and unafraid*, where would you rank yourself when it comes to your boldness in being associated with Christ and sharing the gospel?

Timid									*Unashamed*
1	2	3	4	5	6	7	8	9	10

Describe the reason for your ranking.

Look up the following verses. After each reference, summarize what each passage says about being bold and fearless.

Joshua 1:9

Psalm 27:1

Psalm 27:14

Acts 4:28-29

Romans 8:31

1 Corinthians 16:13

2 Corinthians 3:11-12

Hebrews 13:6

After perusing these Scriptures on courage and boldness, write out a brief prayer to God, asking Him to increase your boldness for Him. Use meaningful phrases from the verses you read to help form your prayer.

Courage is almost a contradiction in terms. It means a strong desire to live, taking the form of a readiness to die.

G. K. CHESTERTON[2]

A MATTER OF LIFE AND DEATH

In Philippians 1:21-26, Paul gives us a glimpse into a question that he pondered in his mind: which was better—to pass on into the next life and be with Christ or to stay in this present one, encouraging others in their faith?

List the reasons he gave for both options.
The benefit of dying:

The benefit of remaining alive:

If you were pondering this choice, what reasons would you give for remaining alive? So you can live long enough to meet the man of your dreams and get married? So you can see your children grow up? So you and your family can finally move into that larger house in a better part of town? Be honest.

Have you ever thought about the benefits other Christians would receive by you remaining alive? List all the reasons you think it is crucial to have close Christian friendships.

Name one or two Christian friends you cannot imagine living life without. After writing their names, list your reasons for choosing them. Do they help you to spiritually progress and find joy in the faith (v. 25)? Explain.

In verse 22, Paul asserted that remaining alive meant he could continue his "fruitful work." How would you describe fruitful work for the gospel?

In the Greek, the phrase *fruitful work* was composed of two words. The word for *fruit*, *karpos*, sometimes meant an actual fruit, but could also mean a figurative fruit such as a deed, action, or result. The Greek word for *work* was *ergon* which means that which is wrought or made. When we fasten these two words together, it gives us a picture of what our marching orders are while on earth. We are to labor in a way that produces spiritual results in the kingdom of God. Our lives should be avenues for the gospel, resulting in personal spiritual growth and spiritual transformation in others. This comes through sharing the gospel so that others may respond and place their faith in Christ as well as discipling fellow believers.

Take a few moments to read the following verses about bearing fruit and working for Christ. As you do, keep in mind that we are *not* saved by any work we do for Christ. We were created to serve Him and do good, but it is not a method that earns our way to heaven.
John 15:8

John 15:16

1 Corinthians 15:58

Ephesians 2:10

Colossians 1:10

1 Thessalonians 5:11-13

Write a summary of what fruitful work for Christ means, based on the preceding verses.

Now it's time for a reality check. Circle the line below that best describes you when it comes to fruitful work.

□ My fruit basket is completely and pitifully empty.
□ There are a couple of pieces of plucked fruit rolling around in the bottom of the basket.
□ I've been busy picking fruit. My basket is just about half full.
□ My fruit basket is overflowing so much that the bottom might fall out.

Are you pleased with your assessment? Explain. How would you like to see this change in the future? List a few adjustments you need to make in your life in order to see more fruitful labor for the Lord.

HEAVENLY MINDED & EARTHLY GOOD

One day in my local church as a young girl, I overheard one of the women of the church talking about a fellow female parishioner. The woman she was speaking of was extremely pious and known by those in the community to be very "religious." She didn't drink, smoke, or swear. No movies or dancing. She would never even think of going shopping on a Sunday. She followed a list of religious dos and don'ts to a T and seemed very judgmental of anyone who didn't also do the same. As I heard the church member speak about this devout lady, she used this phrase: *She is so heavenly minded that she's no earthly good.*

Is this old saying really accurate? Is it possible to be so concerned of the things of heaven that you aren't any good down here on earth? Or instead, had this woman misjudged the other church member, misinterpreting her strict adherence to man-made rules and regulations as being "heavenly minded"? Let's take a peek at what it means to be a Christian with your feet planted here on earth but with heaven on your mind.

Using your own words, paraphrase Philippians 1:27a. (It's written out for you in the CSB version, but write it again using your own words.)
Just one thing: As citizens of heaven, live your life worthy of the gospel of Christ.

How often do you think about the concept of being a citizen of heaven? Place an X on the continuum to display your answer.

Never Rarely Sometimes Often Daily

What are some reasons we as Christians don't keep this concept of our heavenly citizenship at the forefront of our minds?

Paraphrase the rest of verse 27 and all of verse 28.

Then, whether I come and see you or am absent, I will hear about you that you are standing firm in one spirit, in one accord, contending together for the faith of the gospel, not being frightened in any way by your opponents. This is a sign of destruction for them, but of your salvation—and this is from God.

Read the following passage from 1 Peter 4:7-11 that talks about life here on earth drawing to a close. As you do, circle any directive phrases that stand out to you about how we are to live during this time. (Examples: Be sober-minded. Serve others.)

The end of all things is near; therefore, be alert and sober-minded for prayer. Above all, maintain constant love for one another, since love covers a multitude of sins. Be hospitable to one another without complaining. Just as each one has received a gift, use it to serve others, as good stewards of the varied grace of God. If anyone speaks, let it be as one who speaks God's words; if anyone serves, let it be from the strength God provides, so that God may be glorified through Jesus Christ in everything. To him be the glory and the power forever and ever. Amen.

Look back over the passage. What is the total number of words or phrases that you circled?

Review the circled words and phrases. How many of them speak to our treatment of, or our interaction with, others here on earth?

Now use those two numbers to make a fraction. For example, if you circled three phrases and two of them have to do with how we relate to others, your fraction would be $2/3$. What fraction do you come up with?

Does this fraction help you see the importance of how we as Christians treat others? Explain.

What does striving to live out the directives you circled have to do with living a life "worthy of the gospel of Christ" (Phil. 1:27)?

This whole section began with the expression "Just one thing." How would you sum up what one thing we should endeavor to do here on earth because we are citizens of heaven? Craft a catchphrase or motto that will remind you to maintain a heavenly perspective as you deal with others here on earth. Write it below.

ON SOVEREIGNTY AND SUFFERING

Chapter 1 ends by mentioning a part of the Christian life that isn't always easy to swallow—suffering. Read Philippians 1:29-30.

Which aspect of verse 29 would you say is easier for you to do—to believe in Him or to suffer for Him? Explain.

In what ways are believing in Christ and suffering for Him connected?

Has there ever been a time in your walk with God when you suffered, not just in a generic way, but directly due to your faith in Christ? If so, describe briefly what happened.

Read the following verses on suffering carefully. As you do, after each verse jot down any phrases that state why we suffer or what we are to do when we suffer.

VERSE(S)	WHY WE SUFFER	WHAT TO DO WHEN WE SUFFER
Matthew 5:10-12		
Matthew 10:38-39		
Romans 8:17		
2 Thessalonians 1:4-5		
2 Timothy 1:8		
2 Timothy 3:12		
1 Peter 4:12-16		

Have you ever experienced a time of suffering in your life, not necessarily because of your faith, but a time that nonetheless tried your faith? At the time, surely your circumstances were not pleasant. However, looking back, can you now see how God's sovereign hand was in the midst of your suffering? Has it somehow been used to bring about good—either for you or for someone else? In the space provided, take a few moments to describe this situation, sharing both the suffering you incurred and the blessings that God brought out of it.
My suffering situation:

Blessings that came from it:

LIVE IT OUT PRACTICALLY

Bravo for your diligence in wading through the topics and passages covered this week. There have been many! We've contemplated being unashamed and full of courage. We've looked at an important reason for continuing to exist here on earth—so we can be an encouragement to other Christians. We've discussed living as citizens of our true home, heaven, while still physically present in this temporal world. And we have finished off this chapter with a look at suffering. Time now for living out what we have learned.

PREPOSITIONAL LIVING

Do you remember when English class began to be difficult? Oh, it started off innocently enough when we were in grade school. We learned the basic parts of speech. Nouns. Verbs. Adjectives and adverbs. But as each year built upon the previous ones, there were even more parts of speech to learn. Namely, prepositions.

There are approximately one hundred and fifty prepositions in the English language. When I was homeschooling each of my children and they got to around the 7th grade, they were required to memorize the top fifty most common prepositions. I also wanted them to become skilled at identifying them in a sentence.

One day, I was giving my son the technical definition of a preposition (which is "a word governing, and usually preceding, a noun or pronoun and expressing a relation to another word or element in the clause"[3]) when my normally academically quiet husband piped up.

"Why don't you just tell them what my high school English teacher told me?" he interjected. "What was that?" I asked curiously. His reply was a simple rule. He said that his teacher told them that anything a plane can do to a cloud is usually a proposition. It can go through the cloud, under the cloud, around the cloud, it can be in the cloud, with the cloud, and so forth. His suggestion made the light bulb turn on for my children. They rarely had trouble picking out prepositions when diagramming sentences after he gave them this nifty grammar tip.

When we read about our relationship to Christ as Christians, we often see prepositions make an appearance. We experience the grace of God through Christ. We rest in the love of Christ. We are associated with Christ. We are to live for Christ. We experience salvation by Christ's death and resurrection. There are prepositions tethered to so many descriptions of our association with Christ.

Look up the following verses that all use prepositions to depict our affiliation to Jesus. As you do, circle at least one verse that you would like to internalize to help you in your walk with Him.

□ Romans 3:23-24
□ Romans 5:20-21
□ Romans 6:8-11
□ Romans 8:1-2
□ Romans 12:4-5
□ 1 Corinthians 1:9
□ 2 Corinthians 5:17
□ Galatians 3:27

Why did you choose the verse you circled?

Write the verse in the space provided.

What adjustment can you make in your life this week that will enable you to live out the truth of this verse more diligently and effectively?

CHALLENGE OF THE WEEK

If you want an opportunity to put into practice the truths you've learned in this study, complete one of the following challenges. Be ready to share the results of your challenge with your group.

1. **BLESS A FELLOW CHRISTIAN.** In this week's Scripture study, Paul talked about his struggle between dying and being with Christ or remaining alive, which he felt was necessary for the sake of others. Which Christians in your life benefit from you still being alive? Is there someone who looks up to you as a mentor or a teacher? Is there a fellow Christian who gains encouragement or helpful advice from you? Think of a fellow believer to whom you might say as Paul did "… I know that I will remain and continue with ... you for your progress and joy in the faith" (Phil. 1:25). Then do something to bless this person. Drop them a card, email, or a private message on social media encouraging them to continue in their faith. Urge them to stand firm and endure until the end.

2. **LIGHTEN SOMEONE'S LOAD.** In this session we talked a little bit about suffering. Is there someone you know who is suffering either physically, spiritually, or emotionally? Time to put your faith into action. Find ways to help lighten their load. Take a meal. Wash and clean out the interior of their vehicle. Help them perform an outdoor chore or task inside the home. Take them to a doctor's appointment or offer to shuttle their children to activities so that they can have the day off. It doesn't have to be something spectacular. Just coming alongside your friend and helping them in day-to-day living can really boost their spirits.

3. **POST YOUR CATCHPHRASE.** Earlier in this session (on page 44) you came up with a catchphrase or motto to remind yourself to maintain a heavenly perspective as you deal with others here on earth. It was your personal "Just one thing" (Phil. 1:27a). Consider making that catchphrase the screensaver on your phone or writing it on a sticky note to place at your kitchen sink or on your bathroom mirror. If you are feeling more artsy, sketch the catchphrase or motto out, and color it in. You will be sure to be reminded of it every time you see it throughout the day.

MEMORY VERSE

OPTIONAL MEMORY VERSE

Remember that for each lesson, an optional memory verse is provided to further internalize the message of the passages we studied together. To assist you in this endeavor, all six passages are printed in the back of the study guide.

You may want to see if someone else in your group would like to come early or stay a few minutes after your group time so the two of you can practice saying the verses out loud to each other.

The verse for this session is a reminder that although we are living our lives out here on earth, we are true residents of an eternal home.

Just one thing: As citizens of heaven,
live your life worthy of the gospel of Christ.
PHILIPPIANS 1:27a

Just one thing: As citizens of heaven, live your life worthy of the gospel of Christ.

PHILIPPIANS 1:27a

WEEK 3

WHAT MATTERS MOST

LIVING FOR CHRIST & OTHERS

Do nothing out of selfish ambition or conceit, but in humility consider others as more important than yourselves.

PHILIPPIANS 2:3

VIEWER GUIDE

FAVORITE QUOTES

STAND-OUT SCRIPTURES

Video teaching sessions available for purchase at *LifeWay.com/WhatMattersMost*

GROUP GUIDE

ICEBREAKER

What do you remember about getting your high school yearbooks? If your group were to find a picture of you in a yearbook, what would you be doing? Being on a sports team, playing a musical instrument, goofing off in the cafeteria, posing as a member of a club, or participating in an extracurricular activity?

1. *The phrase "thinking the same way" is used often in Philippians. What is the correlation between what you think (your attitude) and having harmonious relationships?*

2. *Why do we tend to put our own wishes over those of others? Do you have a tendency to overlook the desires of someone in your life? Explain.*

3. *Assign someone to read aloud John 15:12-13. What are your thoughts about seeing this familiar passage in a new way—not just giving up your life in a dramatic instant, but "laying down your life" daily by putting others' interests above your own?*

4. *Call on a group member to read aloud Philippians 2:5-11. Identify the phrases in this passage that showcase Christ's attitude—the one Paul told the Philippians to emulate.*

5. *We are told to "do everything without grumbling and arguing" in Philippians 2:14. How has social media made it easier for us to grumble and complain? What characteristics of Christ's humble attitude from question four should we adopt when we interact online?*

6. *Review Philippians 2:14-16. Why do you think Paul used stars to describe Christians in the world? Are you shining brightly? Explain.*

7. *Karen mentioned several people in the Bible who obeyed God when called to go. Do you know any Christians who have done the same—whether called to go around the world or around the block? Have you obeyed in such a way? Explain.*

8. *In Philippians 2:19-30, Paul talked about the character and actions of two trusted, godly friends. Name two godly friends who encourage you and with whom you love serving. How do they make your walk with Christ more joyful?*

ON YOUR OWN

Do you sense God tapping on your heart about sending you somewhere? What are your apprehensions and fears about saying *yes* to His calling? Jot down your thoughts, and then take a minute to pray, asking God for clear direction and courage to do what He asks of you.

PRAYER TIME

Close out your time together by sharing prayer requests related to the topics in this session's study. Then, call on one person to pray.

INTRODUCTION

Recently, my 19-year-old son decided to head out on an adventure. Ever the nature-lover, his plan was to spend a few hours night hiking and stargazing. So he bundled up, grabbed something warm to sip in the car, and drove three hours north to the tip of Michigan's lower peninsula. Now I love the outdoors too. I used to teach preschoolers at a local nature center and enjoyed every minute of it. (Well, except for one unfortunate encounter with a very large snake!) However, since sitting by a toasty warm fire while I sip my warm beverage sounded much better than hiking in the cold, I stayed home.

His final destination was Wilderness State Park, a 10,000-acre lush parcel of land boasting lots of wildlife, including bobcats, mink, muskrats, otters, black bears, and even wolves! It has also been designated a dark sky preserve, a place where there are rules restricting light pollution. This allows the best viewing of the night atmosphere.

While I loved seeing my son so excited to gaze at the heavens that cold January night, my mind kicked into mama mode. I worried about him being all alone—in the dark. Perhaps in the path of a bear who didn't get the memo about hibernating all winter. Maybe instead the beast would wake up wanting a little snack to eat and just happen upon my son munching on some trail mix and decide to eat it—and him! However, since my son is an adult, I couldn't forbid him to go. But we did strike a compromise—he agreed to turn on the "share my location" feature on his phone so I could track where he was at all times. And yes—alert the authorities of his last known location if he failed to return.

He had a glorious time that night simply walking and looking up at the night sky. Because there was no light pollution to dilute the dark, he said the stars and constellations were the most vivid he'd ever seen. Stars shine brightest when they are up against the pure blackness of night.

In this session of our study, Paul declares that Christians shine like stars in the universe, especially when they are placed alongside those whose behavior is dark and sinful. Let's plunge into our study of Philippians 2.

READ IT CAREFULLY

This week we are studying all of Philippians 2. Read through this chapter of Scripture in one sitting or at least over the course of one day. Once you have finished, go back and read it again slowly, soaking in the meaning of this passage. As you do, note the verses that jump out at you and why. Is it because you have a question about a particular verse or segment of Scripture? Does the content encourage you as you face a current situation? Does it convict, inspire, or challenge you? Record the verses that stand out as well as your reasons for choosing them in the space provided.

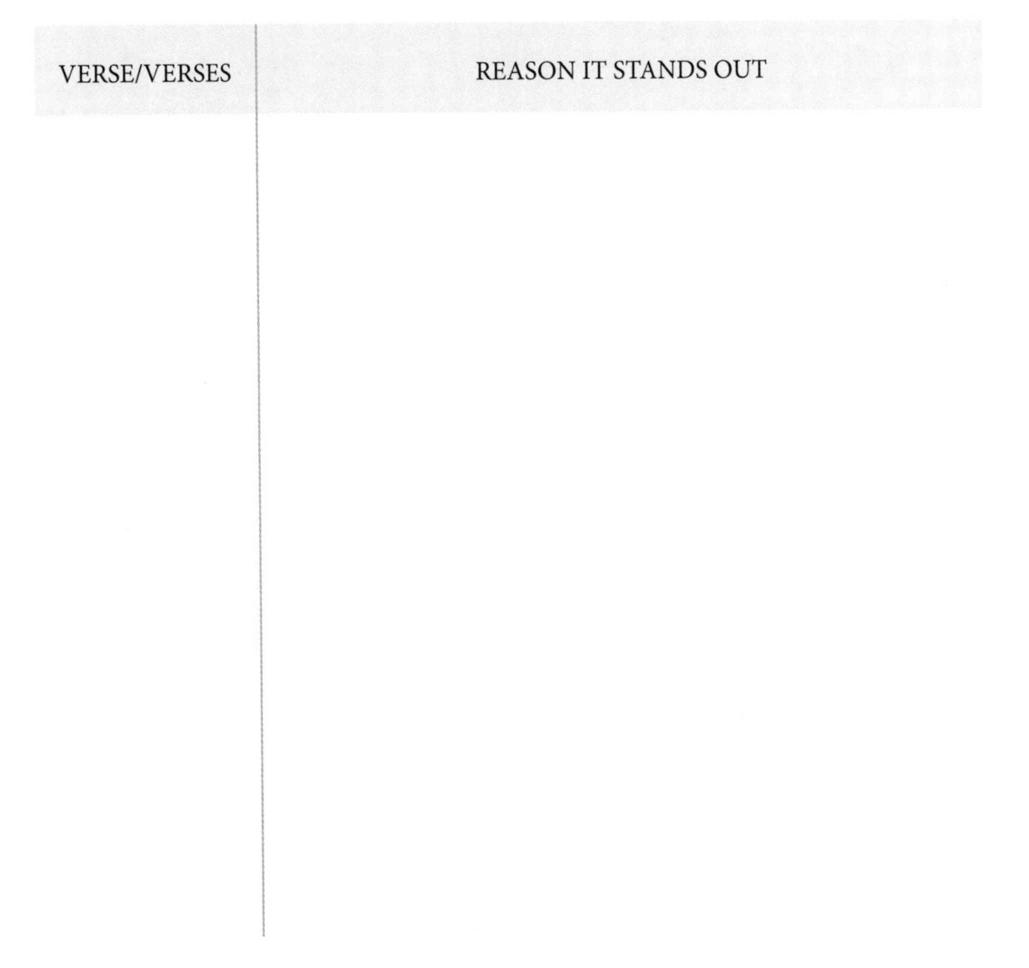

VERSE/VERSES	REASON IT STANDS OUT

Now, go back and place a star beside the verse that most encouraged or challenged you in the text. Then, put a question mark beside the one that most puzzled you.

Continue to add to your list of topics covered in this New Testament letter from Paul. Jot down any subjects mentioned in Philippians 2 along with the corresponding verse reference.

TOPIC	VERSE WHERE IT IS FOUND

Now that you have read these verses carefully, answer the following questions:

Did you discover anything new in this passage you had not noticed in the Bible before? If so, record it here.

Did you spy an old familiar verse in this passage anywhere? If so, which one?

Did you notice any interesting topic covered in this passage you didn't know the Bible covered? If so, what topic?

Good work! Now, spend a little time praying that God will help you internalize this chunk of Scripture and maximize your study of it in the next section as we cover it more in-depth.

STUDY IT PRAYERFULLY

Now let's dive into Philippians 2.

GENUINE HUMILITY

What comes to mind when you think of the concept of *humility*? Is there a particular person whose name blinks upon the screen of your mind? Or maybe you recall seeing an act of heroism that was minimized or a great accomplishment that was downplayed? Just what does it mean to be truly humble?

So often we have an inaccurate view of humility. We determine it means thinking less of ourselves, shying away from any attention, or shooting down what we consider an undeserved compliment. Is this a correct view of humility?

Take a moment right now to jot down a definition of *humility* as you currently understand it. Don't look it up in a dictionary or online; just use your own words.

Humility is:

Now let's see what Philippians has to say about this essential quality of a believer. A problem was lurking under the surface that threatened to divide the church of Philippi. It was the same issue that often divides churches today and distracts them from doing the work of the gospel—*disunity*. This discord is usually filled with and fueled by pride, which is the opposite of humility. There were many layers to the cause of disunity in the Philippian church. We see them here at the beginning of chapter 2.

Read verses 1-2. What words stand out to you about how Christians are supposed to treat each other?

What grade would you give the Christian community to which you are currently connected when it comes to displaying genuine love and being united in spirit and purpose? Write the grade below, anywhere from an A+ to an F.

What specific issues influenced your grade?

Time for a little self-reflection. Look up the following passages and complete the activity that follows.

□ Ephesians 4:1-3
□ Colossians 3:12-15

Let's think for a moment about your behavior in your community of believers. Of the areas listed below, make the following markings:

□ Circle any you struggle with when it comes to relating to the people in your Christian fellowship.
□ Put a box around any that you feel come more naturally for you.
□ Place a star next to the one you most need to work on.

Humility

Patience

Unity

Compassion

Forgiveness

Gentleness

Love

Peace

Kindness

Thankfulness

Now, look back at the topics mentioned above. After each one, write the opposite of the quality listed. For example, the opposite of humility is pride.

Considering only your thoughts and actions, write out a goal stating how you desire to behave in your church and Christian community so as to bring about true unity and display genuine humility.

Look at Philippians 2:3-4. In the Greek, the word translated in English as *humility* means lowly, modest, and cast down. In effect, humbleness of mind. It is noteworthy that the Greek refers to being humble in your mind for it is in the mind where our actions originate. Before people outwardly act in a prideful, cocky, or condescending way, they first form thoughts in their mind of who they are, and those thoughts are far from humble.

Verse 3 also mentions selfish ambition and conceit. These attitudes are in direct opposition to humility. To display authentic humility, you can't be all about yourself, elevating your qualities and capabilities in a conceited way. When we display selfish ambition, we are not trying to advance the gospel; we are trying to advance ourselves. This is pure narcissism.

Godly unity in the body of Christ requires us to think of ourselves properly. This doesn't mean we don't understand, acknowledge, and use our unique strengths, abilities, and spiritual gifts. It just means we do not elevate ourselves over others. We maintain an accurate picture of who we are—and who we are not.

Rewrite verse 4, and personalize it by including a current relationship or situation. Here's an example:
I should not only think about myself when it comes to situations around the office. I should also be thinking of my coworkers' successes and what I might do to help them do their jobs better.

Verse 5 gives us a tall order to fill: "Adopt the same attitude as that of Christ Jesus."

The original word for *attitude* doesn't just refer to our minds. It means the midriff or diaphragm, the parts around the heart.[1] When the Bible speaks of thinking or feeling, often the original language (Hebrew and Greek) refers not only to the heart and mind but also to a person's stomach and digestive system. This concept is problematic to translate into English because it combines both the cognitive and visceral aspects of thinking.[2] It paints a picture of deep-seated emotion or feeling. It's not just knowledge we have parked in our minds; we have deep feelings based on the knowledge we possess.

So, having "the same attitude as that of Christ Jesus" begins in our minds and fleshes itself out in our actions. Let's understand the outlook Paul was referring to here.

Read verses 6-8, and record any phrases that refer to Jesus' attitude and actions. (Hint: There are about half a dozen.)

What was God's response to Christ's actions? Read verses 9-11 and then fill in the blanks with your answers.

God ________ __________ Him, and gave Him the name that is ____________ ____________ ____________. At the name of Jesus, every ___________ will __________ in ____________ and on ____________ and under the ___________. And every tongue will ____________ that Jesus Christ is _______________ ...

What an amazing progression! Because Jesus' attitude was one of pure humility, His actions reflected that humble attitude by casting Himself down. God raised Him up to a place of honor and glory.

I remember being beside myself when homecoming royalty was announced at my son's football game one fall. All but one of the teen boys up for the honor of homecoming king were good-looking, popular, and athletic. They were used to being noticed and to winning many of the activities they tried. They were good kids who were living the good life. However, one boy up for king was just a simple, down-home sort of guy. He wasn't someone you would look at and instantly think he was homecoming royalty by his clothing, appearance, or athletic prowess. But this boy had an amazing attitude. He was kind. Funny. Others-centered. He treated everyone with dignity and honor. He had a humble sweetness about him that made everyone love him. I could hardly contain my

Humility is nothing else but a right judgment of ourselves.

WILLIAM LAW[3]

excitement in the football bleachers when his name was announced as the winner. And what warmed my heart even more was how genuinely happy the other nominees were for him. This boy's humility and genuine kindheartedness brought about exultation in his life as his classmates bestowed upon him the crown of the campus.

Have you ever known someone who displayed a humble attitude and humble actions to be exalted to a place of honor? Briefly describe.

Craft a one- or two-sentence prayer asking God to enable you to adopt a true attitude of humility.

YOU'RE A SHINING STAR

Now, read verses 12 and 13 of chapter 2. Then answer the following questions based on what you read in those verses.

How does Paul refer to the Philippians in verse 12?

Why do you think he told them to obey even more in his absence than when he was with them?

What did Paul tell them to "work out"?

How are they told to work out their salvation?

According to verse 13, who is really doing the working?

What shapes the work God is doing?

The concept of working out your salvation can be a difficult one to understand. Reading verse 12, one might conclude that there is something we can do to bring about our own salvation. A peek into the Greek will show us that this is not true.

The word translated *work out* is the word *katergazomai.* This word means to produce, bring about, or bring to completion. See this phrase as Paul cheering us on in the faith. William Barclay, in his commentary, *The Letters to the Philippians, Colossians, and Thessalonians* says, "It is as if Paul says: 'Don't stop halfway; go on until the work of salvation is fully wrought out in you.' No Christian should be satisfied with anything less than the total benefits of the gospel."[4]

Barclay further explains by urging us to think of man cooperating with God: "The fact is that any gift or any benefit has to be received. A man may be ill and the doctor able to describe the drugs that will cure him; but the man will not be cured until he takes them and he may stubbornly refuse all persuasion to take them. It is so with salvation. The offer of God is there; without it there can be no such thing as salvation. No man can ever receive salvation unless he answers God's appeal and takes what he offers."[5]

In what ways do you think a Christian cooperates with God to bring about the full and "total benefits of the gospel"?

In what ways can our actions and attitudes hinder the complete effect of the gospel in our lives?

Does the phrase "with fear and trembling" throw you for a loop? Does it conjure up an image of being petrified of God because He is unkind or cruel? The word for *fear* means a deep reverence and respect. And the word *trembling*—well, it does mean to shake or quake. So, as we respect and revere God, we do quake a little when we think of His astounding power. We realize at all times in our voyage of faith that God is God, and we are not.

Read Philippians 2:14-18. On a scale of 1 to 10, with 1 being a *total grumbler and complainer* and 10 being *completely cheerful and cooperative*, rank your current attitude.

Grumbler & Complainer *Cheerful & Cooperative*

1 2 3 4 5 6 7 8 9 10

Look up the following verses and, after each one, scrawl out any words or phrases that stand out to you concerning our attitudes, the goodness of God, and our gratefulness to Him.

Ephesians 4:29

Colossians 3:15

1 Thessalonians 5:16-18

Hebrews 12:28-29

James 5:9

1 Peter 4:9

In what area (or areas) of life do you find it the most challenging to refrain from grumbling and complaining?

Time for an attitude adjustment in that area or areas. Fill in the blanks to complete the following sentence, showcasing how you can turn your complaints into contemplating the goodness of God.

In the future, when I am tempted to complain about ____________________, I will instead remember this characteristic of God and be grateful: ____________________________.

Look again at verses 14-16a. Why are we to refrain from grumbling and complaining? How does that bolster our reputation with others?

In contrast, what words are used to describe the generation in which we live?

What does it mean for you to "shine like stars in the world"? Take just a moment to search online for the brightness of a star. What did you discover?

Do you feel like you are shining brightly for Christ and His kingdom? Explain.

What do you think is meant by "hold firm to the word of life" in verse 16?

Paul ends this section in verses 16-18 by talking about the Philippians' faith and his labor on their behalf.

Have you ever had someone—even a child—who you mentored in the faith or to whom you taught the Bible? How does it make your heart feel when you watch that person continue in the faith, living it out loud before others?

TWO FAITHFUL SERVANTS

Let's handle the end of this chapter—verses 19-30—all in one chunk. It speaks of two faithful servants in Paul's life: Timothy and Epaphroditus.

Timothy was the son of Eunice and the grandson of Lois. Both of these women were devoted Christ-followers (2 Tim. 1:5). While Timothy's mother was a Jew, his father was Greek (Acts 16:1). We don't know exactly when or how Timothy became a believer, but we do know that he met Paul when Paul was on his second missionary journey and that they grew to be dear friends. (You can read more about Timothy and Paul in Acts 16–18.)

Peruse Philippians 2:19-30, and then answer the following questions. In verses 19-22, what words are used to describe Timothy?

It is thought that Epaphroditus was the one who took the Letter of Philippians back to the church. Evidently Epaphroditus had been sent by the church to stay in Rome as Paul's personal servant. But while there he became gravely ill, to the point of death. Some scholars think that his illness could well have been the dangerous Roman fever, which took the lives of many at that time in history.[6] It seems that the Philippian church had gotten wind of Epaphroditus's illness.

Paul was afraid that some in the congregation might see Epaphroditus as a quitter since he was returning to them. Not wanting Epaphroditus's home church congregation to feel that he had shirked his responsibilities or not followed through with the mission he was sent to do, Paul took several sentences of the letter to praise his fellow worker and tell the Philippian church that Epaphroditus should be treated with honor, not contempt.

In verses 25-30, what facts are we given about Epaphroditus? Fill in the blanks.

Paul refers to him in five ways:

- ☐ "my ______________"
- ☐ "__________________"
- ☐ "fellow ________________"
- ☐ "your ____________________"
- ☐ "____________________"

How are the Philippians told to treat him in verses 28 through 29?

Verse 30 ends with Paul writing that Epaphroditus was "... risking his life to make up what was lacking in your ministry to me." How does this phrase showcase the concepts of unity, love, fellowship, and purpose covered earlier in the chapter? Does it take more than just one person to help us to grow in our faith in Christ?

How has God used very different people to help you to grow in your faith? Name a few of these people and what character qualities they possessed.

Look back on page 60 where you wrote your definition of *humility*. Now that you have carefully examined the verses in Philippians 2 as well as the other passages we've studied, how would you describe a humble person who is intent on pursuing unity?

LIVE IT OUT PRACTICALLY

This week's lesson has focused on many subjects that are still crucial to the church today: unity, humility, thankfulness, shining like stars in the universe, living out the gospel, and being a faithful servant. Now, let's live out the truths we've learned.

CONTINUING IN THE FAITH

Do you remember your very first job? Your first bona fide, legit employment gig, complete with a paycheck made out in your name?

In my teens and early twenties, I performed many different tasks to earn some pocket change. I nannied children. Washed dishes. Waited tables. Answered phones. But perhaps my favorite job was when I spent two summers at a nature center teaching classes for four-year-olds.

I learned how to identify critters in the pond, how to tell a chipmunk from a thirteen-lined ground squirrel, and—of utmost importance—how to spot poison ivy. (*Leaves of three? Then, let it be!*)

My poison ivy identification skills have come in handy over the years. One time, a friend suspected she had it growing all over her shed. Upon inspection, I discovered she was right. So, her family took care to remove it, wearing long sleeves and gloves for protection.

However, she mentioned a frightening fact to me about their removal process. She said they'd burned all the ivy in a giant bonfire while they stood over it roasting marshmallows. While my friend knew the danger of touching the ivy itself, it hadn't occurred to her that burning the plant—emitting smoke that had the plant's oils mingled in it—would cause a worse reaction than just touching the leaves.

Sure enough, her whole family acquired blistering rashes, especially on their faces. And their eyes became sorely bloodshot and painfully itchy. One son even developed a serious respiratory reaction. All this occurred because she only knew half the truth about poison ivy—touching it is bad. She didn't know that burning it while standing nearby is even worse.

John 8:31-32 states, "Then Jesus said to the Jews who had believed him, 'If you continue in my word, you really are my disciples. You will know the truth, and the truth will set you free.'" Here we see mentioned Jews who "had believed" Jesus. This doesn't mean they had fully committed to Him. Authentic faith is continued and constant. The beginning of our walk with God is only half of the story. We can't stop there. We must continue to allow God to grow our faith.

While our faith's start is crucial, we must know and live the rest of the story. We must keep growing in Christ, continually walking in God's Word in a way that sets us free and keeps sin from poisoning our lives and causing a mighty—even painful—mess. We must work out our salvation with fear and trembling, just as Philippians 2:12-13 urges us to.

Continuing in God's Word doesn't mean just learning religious concepts. It means experiencing the actual truth of God's Word in a totally transformational way. In fact, the original Greek word for *know* in John 8:32 doesn't suggest tucking away ideas in our minds. It constitutes genuine action on our part. It means to recognize, realize, ascertain, and to come to properly understand a truth through personal, firsthand experience.

We don't properly understand by skimming the Bible, but by intentionally internalizing its truths, applying them to real-life situations, and forging our faith solidly as we continually experience Jesus and His saving grace firsthand.

Like the old saying goes, we need to get into God's Word so His Word can get into us.

Determine today not just to rely on the fact of a past salvation experience, but forge ahead in your faith. Continue to grow in His Word. We need the whole truth of the gospel. Jesus saved us (past tense), but He is continually perfecting us too (present tense), if only we will cooperate.

Dig into the truth of the Scriptures for yourself, rather than just relying on assumptions and someone's stories. When you really know the truth—in the true biblical sense—you can live it out in a way that ushers in authentic freedom.

About which subjects of Scripture do you feel you might only know partial truths? List a few of them here:

Begin to discover more about Scripture by taking a few moments now to search for various words and phrases in a concordance, a key word list in the back of your Bible, or in an online Bible. Record truths, thoughts, and questions as you dig in.

Isn't this a glorious thought? We can know the truth. The truth sets us free.

How? "If you continue in my word" (John 8:31b).

Keep on continuing.

CHALLENGE OF THE WEEK

If you want even more opportunity to put into practice the truths you've learned in this lesson, complete one of the following challenges. Be ready to share the results of your challenge with your group.

1. **LIVE THE SCRIPTURE.** Think of a practical way to live out the truth of Philippians 2:3-4:

   Do nothing out of selfish ambition or conceit, but in humility consider others as more important than yourselves. Everyone should look out not only for his own interests, but also for the interests of others.

   Perhaps you will place the interest of your spouse before your own by cooking his favorite meal, even though it's food you really don't care for. Or maybe you will participate in a child's favorite activity that isn't something you are even remotely interested in. Or you'll go to that sappy, tear-jerking movie with a friend although you'd rather have a root canal.

   On the neighboring page, list a few ideas for putting the interests of another first. Then, follow through on at least one of the ideas in the next week.

2. **TAKE THE "NO GRUMBLING PLEDGE."** For the next seven days, banish grumbling from your speech. No whining when tackling chores around the house. No complaining about a task at work or an assignment at church. Don't even roll your eyes at your spouse when you clean up a mess he made. No. Grumbling. Allowed. See if banishing complaining from your life for a week makes you more joyful.

3. **ENCOURAGE THE DIFFICULT ONE.** This is for the brave of heart. Is there a fellow believer with whom you have had a hard time getting along in the past? Write them an encouraging note, pointing out at least one aspect of their personality or an action they have taken that you appreciate. End the note by telling them how grateful you are that they are a fellow Christian and letting them know you prayed for them that day. Don't forget to actually pray for them!

MEMORY VERSE

OPTIONAL MEMORY VERSE

Remember that for each lesson, there is an optional memory verse provided to further drive home the significance of the passages we've studied together. To make this easier for you, all six passages are printed in the back of the study guide.

You may want to see if someone else in your group would like to come early or stay a few minutes after your group time so the two of you can practice saying the verses out loud to each other.

The verse for this session challenges us to live in a way that puts others first.

Do nothing out of selfish ambition or conceit, but in humility consider others as more important than yourselves.
PHILIPPIANS 2:3

Do nothing out of selfish ambition or conceit, but in humility consider others as more important than yourselves.

PHILIPPIANS 2:3

WEEK 4

WHAT MATTERS MOST

HOW & WHY WE RUN THE RACE

Brothers and sisters, I do not consider myself to have taken hold of it. But one thing I do: Forgetting what is behind and reaching forward to what is ahead, I pursue as my goal the prize promised by God's heavenly call in Christ Jesus.

PHILIPPIANS 3:13-14

VIEWER GUIDE

FAVORITE QUOTES

STAND-OUT SCRIPTURES

Video teaching sessions available for purchase at *LifeWay.com/WhatMattersMost*

GROUP GUIDE

ICEBREAKER

Paul likens the Christian life to running a race. What are your thoughts on running? Did you run track back in high school? Are you currently a runner? Or are you the kid who feigned sickness on the day everyone had to run a mile in gym class?

1. *Review Philippians 3:1-6. What were Paul's religious credentials, and what religious credentials might a Christian boast about today?*

2. *Do you know someone, or a group of people, whose beliefs promote the wrong equation of Jesus + _________ = Salvation? What do they put in the blank?*

3. *Sometimes the hardest people to share the gospel with are those who are already living a good, moral life. Have you ever tried to talk about faith in Christ with such a person? If so, what tips or ideas would you give for having this kind of conversation?*

4. *Paul made it clear in Philippians 3 that knowing Christ was the priority of his life. Can you say the same? Why or why not? If knowing Christ is your life's priority, how does that change the way you live?*

5. *Review Philippians 3:13-14. It seems like Paul rolls two things—forgetting what is behind and then reaching forward to what is ahead—into one action. Why could it be counterproductive to just do half of that equation, either forgetting the past but not reaching forward or trying to move ahead while still dwelling on the past?*

6. *Why is it so difficult sometimes to forget what is behind us? Do you personally struggle with this? Explain. Share any practical actions you have discovered that help you forget the past and press on. (Example: Karen deleting the Timehop app from her phone.)*

7. *In Philippians 3:15-21, Paul mentioned both good and bad examples of people he'd encountered. One type was to be avoided. The other kind was to be emulated. Who do you know that lives a Christlike life worth imitating? Are you living such a life? Explain.*

ON YOUR OWN

Is there a personal sin situation from your past that's keeping you from moving forward? Briefly describe it here. Spend a few moments confessing this sin to God and asking Him for forgiveness. Then, based on Psalm 103:12, write "As far as the east is from the west" across the description, signifying how far God has removed your sin from you through the finished work of Jesus on the cross.

PRAYER TIME

End your time together by taking prayer requests related to the topics in this week's session. Then call on one person to pray for your group.

INTRODUCTION

For the last two decades, I have been a proud sports mom. I've spent oodles of hours parked on a metal bleacher, wooden bench, or in a nylon lawn chair, cheering on one of my children. I had a daughter who played softball and volleyball, and two sons who were baseball and football players. My sons also dabbled a bit in soccer and golf. As a result, I have hooted and hollered, baked color-coordinated team snacks, and watched two of my children win state championships in football and basketball and one son win a baseball world series twice! (I guess I forgot to mention that I'm also a bragging sports mama!) However, one sport I never got into was ice hockey. Even though it is popular in my home state of Michigan, none of my children played it, so it wasn't on my radar.

Ice hockey is a fast-paced and highly emotional sport. It can also turn somewhat violent in a heartbeat. People sometimes joke that they went to a fight and a hockey game broke out. Oh my! Due to the small, black disc that catapults across the ice at lightning speed, hockey players need to keep their eyes open and their reaction times fast. However, it isn't enough to just have a quick in-the-moment reaction time. Hockey players need to learn to think ahead, anticipating where that puck will fly next.

One of professional hockey's biggest legends is Wayne Gretzky. In fact, his nickname is *The Great One*. This native Canadian's career spanned over two decades. He played for a half dozen teams, finishing out his career in the National Hockey League playing for the New York Rangers. Gretzky was known for many motivating quotes, but the following is my favorite—words of wisdom his dad passed down to him. It gives us a peek into the reason for his immense success in the game. Wayne's dad used to tell him to "Go where the puck is going ... not where it's been."[1]

This renowned athlete practiced a crucial strategy in his sport. You must think forward. You can't determine your course of action based on where the puck has been. You need to intentionally and accurately anticipate where the puck is going next to achieve success. Winning hockey games necessitates forward-thinking.

As Christians, we must also be forward-thinking. We cannot idle our brains in the past, whether by exalting in the good times of glory days gone by or by beating ourselves up over regretful choices that lead us to a place of sorrow. We must choose to forget the past and press forward to the future, eyes fixed firmly on Christ. We will learn just how to do that in Philippians 3 as Paul reveals more truths on how and why we run the race of faith.

READ IT CAREFULLY

In this session, we will cover all of Philippians 3. Read through this portion of Scripture in one sitting or at least over the course of one day. Once you have finished, go back and read it again slowly, soaking in the meaning of this passage. As you do, note the verses that jump out at you and why. Is it because you have a question about that particular verse or segment of Scripture? Does the content encourage you as you face a current situation? Does it convict, inspire, or challenge you? Record the verses that stand out, as well as your reasons for choosing them, in the spaces provided.

VERSE/VERSES	REASON IT STANDS OUT

Now, go back and place a star beside the verse that most encouraged or challenged you in the text. Then put a question mark beside the one that most puzzled you.

Continue your running list of the topics covered in Philippians. Jot down any subjects mentioned in chapter 3 along with the corresponding verse reference.

TOPIC	VERSE WHERE IT IS FOUND

Now that you have read these verses carefully, answer the following questions:

Did you discover anything new in this passage you had not noticed in the Bible before? If so, record it here.

Did you spy an old familiar verse in this passage anywhere? If so, which one?

Did you notice any interesting topic covered in this passage you didn't know the Bible covered? If so, what topic?

Good work! Now, spend a little time praying that God will help you internalize this chunk of Scripture and maximize your study of it in the next section as we cover it more in-depth.

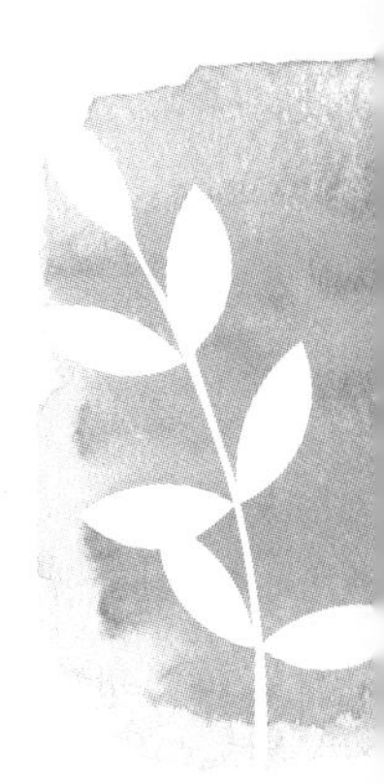

STUDY IT PRAYERFULLY

Now that you've carefully read the passage for this week, it is time to study it verse-by-verse to excavate the intended meaning and the useful application.

FINDING TRUE JOY IN JESUS

In Philippians 3:1, Paul urged his friends, "In addition, my brothers and sisters, rejoice in the Lord. To write to you again about this is no trouble for me and is a safeguard for you." The Greek word for *rejoice* is the word *chairō,* and it means to be cheerful, find gladness, and delight. Traditionally it is also tied to the concept of grace and a word meaning leaning toward.

We do tend to lean toward that which we think will make us happy, don't we?

Consider the following popular phrases and sayings. Underline or highlight any you have heard before that talk about joy and happiness.

- The surest way to happiness is to lose yourself in a cause much greater than yourself.[2]
- Happiness is like a butterfly; the more you chase it, the more it will elude you, but if you turn your attention to other things, it will come and sit softly on your shoulder. —Henry David Thoreau[3]
- To get the full value of joy you must have someone to divide it with. —Mark Twain[4]
- Don't let someone else hold the key to your happiness.
- Happiness is a state of mind.
- Happiness is a warm puppy. —Charles M. Schulz[5]

Contrast these sayings with what Paul wrote in the first verse of chapter 3. He urges us to rejoice in the Lord. Do any of the previous statements speak to rejoicing in the Lord?

What do you think it means to rejoice in the Lord? Don't look it up, just give your thoughts off the top of your head.

When you consider the concept of joy being tied to grace, and note that the root word of *rejoice* means *to lean toward something*, how does this help clarify your thoughts about what it means to rejoice in the Lord?

Look up the following verses. Note what each one says about joy and rejoicing in the Lord.
Psalm 5:11

Psalm 16:11

Psalm 21:6

Psalm 32:7

Psalm 34:5

Psalm 51:12

Psalm 59:16

Acts 13:47-49

Romans 5:10-11

How did these Scriptures help you better understand what it means to rejoice in the Lord?

Perhaps your last answer mentioned being in God's presence or pondering your salvation. Do you feel these two concepts are tied to true joy? If so, how? Can you think of any specific examples from your own life or someone else's life?

It is important to note that Paul wrote with great certainty about true Christian joy, even though he was in prison. Being a follower of Jesus in the Philippian church meant the possibility of facing threats, persecution, even death. Despite these realities, Paul was confident that they, like he, could experience joy in the Lord because of the certainty of their salvation and God's constant presence through the Holy Spirit. What unspeakable joy indeed!

RELIGIOUS BOASTING VERSUS KNOWING CHRIST

Read verses 2-6 carefully. Paul's writing seems to take a rather sharp and sudden turn. He pivots from talking about joy to warning the Philippians of the wicked teachers lurking and working in the church. He refers to them as "dogs" and "evil workers."

What do you think was going on?

Paul was calling out those who were contradicting his teaching about salvation. While he was teaching that salvation comes from grace alone and that there is nothing anyone can do to earn salvation, these false teachers, called Judaizers, were adding something to the salvation equation. They taught that in addition to responding to the gospel in faith, if someone desired to be saved, they must conform to the Jewish law. This included—if you were a male—being circumcised.

Paul's description of the false teachers was sharp, calling them "dogs," "evil workers," and "those who mutilate the flesh" (v. 2). You can hear in his words his protective care for the church and his anger toward those who were trying to lead the people astray. Paul knew that adhering to the Jewish laws, rules, and regulations had nothing to do with salvation. It was and is by faith alone. Through Christ alone. It is God's gracious gift to us.

To dismiss the false teachers, who Paul said were putting "confidence in the flesh," Paul clearly laid out all of the reasons he had to boast in his flesh—his heritage, his behavior, and his adherence to the rules and rituals of the Jewish faith. His credentials far exceeded those of the false teachers.

Look again at Philippians 3:3-6, and then fill in the blanks.

"... although I have reasons for confidence in the __________. If anyone else thinks he has grounds for confidence in the flesh, I have __________: __________________ the __________ day; of the nation of __________, of the tribe of __________________, a __________ born of __________; regarding the law, a __________; regarding zeal, persecuting the __________; regarding the righteousness that is in the law, ________________."

Have you encountered any modern-day teachers, or perhaps even people you know, who attempt to add to the salvation equation? Perhaps they say following certain rules about how you dress, what you eat, or what activities you engage in is intrinsic to salvation and if you stray from their rules and regulations you are not a true Christian.

Can you think of any such people? And what do they say you must do to gain salvation? Fill in the chart below with any actions, attitudes, or rules that modern-day false teachers and misguided Christians might say are signs of true salvation.

	A CHRISTIAN WHO IS TRULY SAVED
ALWAYS	
NEVER	
DOES	
DOESN'T	
DRESSES	
BELIEVES	
THINKS	
NEVER ASSOCIATES WITH	

Read through the following verses listed below that speak of salvation. Then answer the question that follows them.

□ Psalm 62:1
□ John 3:16-17
□ John 6:47
□ Acts 4:12
□ Romans 10:9-10
□ 2 Timothy 1:9-10

Based on the preceding verses, what would you say to someone who asks how a person receives salvation, securing an eternal home in heaven with Jesus?

After Paul listed the many reasons for which he could have confidence in the flesh, he switched to speaking of the only true reason to have confidence in our salvation at all—knowing Christ Jesus. Read verses 7-11.

How does Paul now view his vast religious achievements?

They now are considered as a loss to him because of what?
Fill in the blanks.
The ______________ of knowing ________________.

In verse 8, Paul gives a rather graphic description of what he now thinks of his past achievements and accolades. You may want to look up Philippians 3:8 in a few different versions of the Bible to get an accurate picture.

What does he call them?

Some versions referred to these things as *garbage*. Others say *rubbish*. The actual Greek word is *skybalon,* and this is its only appearance in all of Scripture. Its meaning points to two substances. First, it refers to refuse—those unwanted and worthless scraps of peelings and pits that are thrown to the dogs. But it also can mean that which comes out of the dogs after they have digested the scraps. *Yikes!* (In fact, some versions of the Bible translate this word as *dung*.) It appears that Paul was trying to think of the most worthless object on earth to describe the accomplishments and qualities he used to boast about and find glory in.

What does this tell you about how we should view our own religious accomplishments or accolades? How are we to view them in comparison to the glorious privilege of knowing Jesus Christ?

Using what you read in verses 8-10, write in the missing words below that state what Paul teaches us concerning knowing Christ.

I will gain Christ and be ________ in Him.

This doesn't mean having a _______________ of my own from the law.

It does mean having one that is through __________ in Christ—the __________________ from God based on faith.

My goal is to ________ Him and the _______ of His resurrection.

I also want to experience the __________________ of His sufferings.

I also long to be conformed to His __________.

If someone were to ask you what your life goals are, would you have rattled off any of the above statements? Do you truly long to know Christ, even to the point of sharing in His sufferings? Consider these questions and journal your thoughts in the space provided.

How often would you say you ponder this concept of knowing Christ so intimately that you identify with His sufferings and even His death?

Never Rarely Sometimes Often Daily

Why do you think we Christians don't ponder this concept more often? Keep in mind that Christians in this area of the world during Paul's day were not always welcomed with open arms. They faced ridicule, persecution, and sometimes even death. Contrast that with the cushy Christianity most of us experience today. We might think persecution is when the department store clerk doesn't wish us "Merry Christmas!" when we are buying stocking stuffers for our children. Or when someone expresses that they don't like us because we are churchgoers, and they don't believe in God. So, why is "share in the fellowship of Christ's suffering" not usually on our goals list?

ON FORGETTING AND FORGING FORWARD

My kids went all crazy when I got my first smartphone. I was perfectly content with my old flip phone model. I could send and receive calls. I could even text on it, although it took a while. But one day after saving my pennies and being wooed to another company that offered a deal too good to pass up, I joined the ranks of the smartphone owners of the world.

My kids wasted no time in downloading all sorts of cool apps they thought I couldn't live without. There were some designed to make my budgeting more organized. Others made my grocery shopping streamlined. There were photo editing applications and social media shortcuts. And one of the apps they thought I simply must have was called Timehop. And so, they scrolled and tapped their way to this nifty little gimmick and put it on my phone.

Timehop allows you a peek into your past. Based on whatever day of the year it is currently, it pulls up pictures and statuses you posted from that same day in past years. At first I found it sort of fun when I spied the little aqua green dinosaur on my phone taking me on a Timehop. I could see what I was doing, and whom I was hanging out with, one, two, or three years ago on that same day. But after a while, this time travel tool began to make me gloomy.

Sometimes it brought up pictures of my sister-in-law, who passed away from breast and bone cancer a short while ago. Other times, it brought up pictures of my husband and me hanging out with some couples from church or our circle of friends. One morning, as I looked at the picture of the smiling folks there on my screen, I realized that two of the couples in that picture are now divorced. At other times, I would be met in the morning with the picture of a former friend of mine, someone with whom my friendly relationship had now become fractured.

I soon sent the Timehop app to the trash.

Looking back can sometimes knock us off course for the future. It doesn't have to be a sad moment from our past. Often looking back at happier times or past accomplishments can leave us in a state of despondency as well. Paul addressed the concept of looking too closely at our past in the last part of Philippians 3.

Read Philippians 3:12-14. Rephrase the passage into your own words.

Paul makes it clear he has not achieved perfection here on earth. He already addressed not having achieved it with his human efforts or his religious strivings in the past. And here he claims just knowing Christ and obtaining the gift of salvation does not make him perfect here on earth either.

However, he does say that there is just one thing he does. It is a two-step process. What is it?

__________________ what is behind.
__________________ ________________ to what is ahead.

How often would you say you dwell on the past? Underline or highlight the word or phrase in the following list that most accurately describes you.

- ☐ I never dwell on the past.
- ☐ On rare occasions I might park my mind in the past, but not too often.
- ☐ I would say that periodically I do think about the past, but it is not a weekly occurrence.
- ☐ I do idle my brain in past experiences and relationships often.
- ☐ My mind, heart, and emotions are so tightly tethered to the past that it is almost debilitating.

Being emotionally handicapped due to circumstances and relationships in our past is a relatively common phenomenon. Many people seek the help of a counselor or psychologist to work through something that happened to them at an earlier time in their lives.

For some of us, we can't shake the thought that we might not be forgiven for something we did to someone. Others of us have a hard time forgiving someone who offended, hurt, or greatly violated us. Or, even more often, we can't seem to forgive ourselves for a past choice or action. But forgiveness issues aren't the only ones that trip us up.

Perhaps a change of roles or season of life leaves us depressed and debilitated. Perhaps we no longer are employed at that company or we don't have the pleasure of having little children in our home anymore. Maybe it's giving up something else we dearly loved.

Is there something that often tethers you to the past? If so, briefly describe it here.

Look up the following passages, and then jot down your thoughts to the subsequent questions.

In this first passage, the Lord has just called Moses to lead the Hebrews out of their Egyptian captivity. But look at Moses's response.

Read Exodus 4:10-13. Can you relate to Moses? When you sense God is calling you to do something for Him, do you point to your past and the weaknesses you have struggled with as an excuse not to do what He is asking you to do? Can you think of a specific incident where this was the case? Briefly describe it here.

How can knowing that God did indeed use Moses to lead His people out of captivity help you not to use your past weaknesses as an excuse for disobedience?

This next chunk of Scripture describes God's actions in delivering the rebellious nation of Israel out of captivity. Read it, and then answer the questions that follow.

Read Isaiah 43:16-19. What does God command us to do with the past?

What does God say about the future? How are His words comforting and encouraging?

"Go back?" he thought. "No good at all! Go sideways? Impossible! Go forward? Only thing to do! On we go!" So up he got, and trotted along with his little sword held in front of him and one hand feeling the wall, and his heart all of a patter and a pitter.

J. R. R. TOLKIEN[6]

The final passage talks about our lives prior to salvation.

Read Galatians 4:7-9. List words or phrases that describe what we were like before we knew Christ.

Now list any descriptions that talk about our current lives as Christians.

How do you answer Paul's question, *Do you want to be enslaved all over again to things of your past nature?*

Read Philippians 3:15-17. What word does Paul use to describe people who think in the manner he has been urging them to in the prior verses—forgetting their past and pressing forward to the future?

In the English language, we might think of the word *mature* as meaning older and wiser. The Greek word that is used here, *teleios*, means full grown, perfected, or complete as it relates to Christian character. In verse 17, Paul urges the Philippians to imitate him in his maturity. He is not saying this arrogantly. Rather he knows he has grown to the level in his walk with Christ where he is living out the truth he's sharing. So he said with confidence, *If you want to know how to live the Christian life. Just watch me.* Paul also knows there are other believers living in such a way and urged the Philippians to model them as well.

Do you know people who quietly but confidently live out their faith in such a way that you want to imitate them as they imitate Christ? If so, who?

Are you at a place in your walk with Christ where you could humbly but confidently say to another believer "Imitate me"? Explain.

Now, finish up by reading Philippians 3:18-21. What words and phrases does Paul pen to describe the evil people he is referring to?

Here Paul was moved to tears as he considered those who lived "as enemies of the cross." There is debate over whom Paul was referring to. Some scholars think Paul was talking again about the Judaizers. However, other Bible scholars believe Paul was referring to a particular party of the men known as Gnostics. The term *gnostic* derives from *gnosis*, which in Greek means knowledge. This sect believed that they were privy to a secret knowledge about divine matters.

The Gnostics were heretics—people who distorted the gospel and practiced a false religion. They tried to make Christianity a highly intellectualized philosophy. They believed that there were two realities. First, anything that related to the spirit was good. But on the flipside, they thought that anything that pertained to matter was inherently evil. Due to this belief, sin abounded in the camp of the Gnostics.

Since they thought that all matter was evil, they felt it didn't matter at all what you did with matter—including the body. You could eat whatever you wanted. Have sex with whomever you wanted. Drink as much as you wanted. You had freedom to satisfy your desires. Paul was calling them out for contorting noble and good things to justify participating in heinous sins.

But now look at the contrast in Philippians 3:20-21. How does Paul describe believers? Answer by completing the following sentences.

Believers' true citizenship is in ____________. They ____________ wait for a Savior from there, the Lord Jesus Christ. He will ______________ the body of our ____________ condition into the likeness of His ___________ body. He will do this by the __________ that enables Him to subject _____________ to Himself.

Using a physical dictionary or an online source, look up the definition to the following two words.
Humble (meaning lowly):

Glorious:

Look up the following Scriptures, and jot down anything you learn about our future, glorified bodies.
John 11:26

Romans 8:10-11

2 Corinthians 5:1-5

Revelation 21:4

What crosses your mind when you think of your lowly body being exchanged for a glorious body in Christ's likeness?

LIVE IT OUT PRACTICALLY

We have taken a close look at many of the topics covered in Philippians 3. We know what type of people to watch out for—those who would add something to the salvation equation, who would lead others astray, and who are enemies of the cross of Christ. We've pondered leaving our pasts behind and pressing forward to the future. And most of all, we've pored over the verses telling us how to really know Christ. Time now to live out practically what we have learned.

LEAVING IT IN THE REARVIEW MIRROR

Forgetting the past is not easy. Nor is it something to be discussed flippantly. While I've had a hard time parting with certain relationships, circumstances, and events in my past, I'm sure many of you have much deeper hurts and difficult situations to put behind you. The last thing I would want to do is suggest you can easily forget the past by answering a few questions over a ten-minute span. I know that's not possible. For some it may take months, years, even decades to completely move forward. Often deep counsel is needed to allow you to be free from something you did or something that happened to you in the past. Please know if that is you, I am praying fervently for you as we do this next exercise.

Think of just one relationship, circumstance, or event in your past that seems to hinder your current progress, holding you back from what God has for you and your future. Briefly write about it in the space provided.

How have you tried dealing with this issue? Describe what you have done to push past this stumbling block.

Have you talked with anyone at length about this issue? If not, consider getting wise counsel either from a mature Christian, a member of your church's pastoral staff, or a licensed biblical counselor.

Read the following verses carefully and slowly. You may even want to read them out loud. Put a star beside one passage to meditate on in the next few minutes as you ask God to help you to leave the past behind and press forward into what He has for you in the future.

When I can't forgive myself:

I have been crucified with Christ, and I no longer live, but Christ lives in me. The life I now live in the body, I live by faith in the Son of God, who loved me and gave himself for me.

GALATIANS 2:20

Therefore, if anyone is in Christ, he is a new creation; the old has passed away, and see, the new has come! Everything is from God, who has reconciled us to himself through Christ and has given us the ministry of reconciliation. That is, in Christ, God was reconciling the world to himself, not counting their trespasses against them, and he has committed the message of reconciliation to us.

2 CORINTHIANS 5:17-19

When I have a hard time forgiving someone else:

Therefore, you should pray like this: Our Father in heaven, your name be honored as holy. Your kingdom come. Your will be done on earth as it is in heaven. Give us today our daily bread. And forgive us our debts, as we also have forgiven our debtors. And do not bring us into temptation, but deliver us from the evil one. For if you forgive others their offenses, your heavenly Father will forgive you as well. But if you don't forgive others, your Father will not forgive your offenses.

MATTHEW 6:9-15

On forging ahead despite the way I've been treated by others in the past:

Do not be agitated by evildoers; do not envy those who do wrong. For they wither quickly like grass and wilt like tender green plants. Trust in the LORD and do what is good; dwell in the land and live securely. Take delight in the LORD, and he will give you your heart's desires. Commit your way to the LORD; trust in him, and he will act, making your righteousness shine like the dawn, your justice like the noonday. Be silent before the LORD and wait expectantly for him; do not be agitated by one who prospers in his way, by the person who carries out evil plans. Refrain from anger and give up your rage; do not be agitated—it can only bring harm. For evildoers will be destroyed, but those who put their hope in the LORD will inherit the land.

PSALM 37:1-9

CHALLENGE OF THE WEEK

If you want even more opportunity to put into practice the truths you've learned in this lesson, choose to do one of the following challenges. Be ready to share the results of your challenge with your group.

1. THANK YOUR EXAMPLE. Think of someone who has been a great example to you in the faith, someone worthy of being imitated because of his or her Christian character. Take the time to thank them for the great example they have been to you in your walk with Christ. Send them a private message on social media. Call them on the phone. Write them a handwritten letter. Or better yet, if they live nearby, take them out and treat them to coffee or a meal as you tell them face-to-face what a fabulous example they have been to you.

2. TAKE A "JOY RIDE" (OR WALK). Use a phone app such as Spotify® or Pandora® to search for songs about being joyful in the Lord. Play them on your phone as you take a scenic drive somewhere in the country. Or, if weather permits, pop in some earphones and take a joy walk. Listen to the songs as you travel, expressing your gratefulness to God for the joy He brings to your life, despite your earthly circumstances. Sometimes purposefully focusing on what we are grateful for will help us experience the true joy of the Lord.

3. TAKE A TRIP DOWN MEMORY LANE. Find a time and place to be alone with just your Bible, a notebook or journal, and two pens—one of them red. Spend a few prayerful moments asking God to help you to take a trip down memory lane, even though it might be painful. Your goal is to identify situations or people in your past that are hindering your current and future growth.

   Using the non-red pen, sketch out a timeline beginning with the year you were born and ending with the current year. Make sure to leave plenty of room, marking off the different decades of your life. The final marking may only be a partial decade depending on your current age. As you ponder the timeline, place an X on any year where something happened that you still have a hard time dealing with today.

   Underneath the X, briefly describe the situation. Then, using the red pen, draw a line through that description and underneath it write the words "God saw and He cares." Use an online resource such as BibleGateway.com to look up any Scriptures that apply to your situation. Write the Scripture references below the description of your situation. Prayerfully look over this timeline for the next few days, asking God to help you release the situations and people that seem to hold your soul hostage.

MEMORY VERSE

OPTIONAL MEMORY VERSE

Remember that for each lesson, there is an optional memory verse provided to further internalize the message of the passages we've studied together. To assist you in this endeavor, all six passages are printed in the back of the study guide.

You may want to see if someone else in your group would like to come early or stay a few minutes after your group time so the two of you can practice saying the verses out loud to each other.

The verse for this session is an admonition to press on and not stay stuck in the past.

Brothers and sisters, I do not consider myself to have taken hold of it. But one thing I do: Forgetting what is behind and reaching forward to what is ahead, I pursue as my goal the prize promised by God's heavenly call in Christ Jesus.

PHILIPPIANS 3:13-14

Brothers and sisters, I do not consider myself to have taken hold of it. But one thing I do: Forgetting what is behind and reaching forward to what is ahead, I pursue as my goal the prize promised by God's heavenly call in Christ Jesus.

PHILIPPIANS 3:13-14

WEEK 5

WHAT MATTERS MOST

TURNING WORRY INTO WORSHIP

Don't worry about anything, but in everything, through prayer and petition with thanksgiving, present your requests to God. And the peace of God, which surpasses all understanding, will guard your hearts and minds in Christ Jesus.

PHILIPPIANS 4:6-7

VIEWER GUIDE

FAVORITE QUOTES

STAND-OUT SCRIPTURES

GROUP GUIDE

ICEBREAKER

What amount of time do you spend worrying about something or someone on a daily basis? Has this percentage of time changed over the years? If so, why?

1. *Philippians 4 begins with a call to stand firm. Karen mentioned that in order to stand firm we must first know how to walk in faith, using both our "faith" foot as well as our "walk" foot. Do you tend to be more in the "go-getter" group who uses only the walk foot or the "God's got this" gang that uses the faith foot? Why is it important to use both feet?*

2. *Why is it important for brothers and sisters in the faith to get along? Can you think of a time when a strained relationship in the church affected its witness? Explain. (Be careful to give general details and refrain from using any names.)*

3. *Call on someone to read aloud Philippians 4:4-5. What are some things we, as Christians, allow to steal our joy? Which of the things we listed affects you the most? Explain.*

4. *How does knowing "the Lord is near"—in proximity and in returning—help you find joy?*

5. *Review Philippians 4:6-7. What is something you are currently worried about? How are you praying about the situation? How can you express thanks in the midst of your praying?*

6. *Enlist three people to read aloud Philippians 4:8 from different translations of the Bible. Then answer this question: Of the eight things mentioned, which one is the most difficult for you to dwell on? Why?*

7. *How does the thought that God is not worried help you be free from anxiety as well?*

ON YOUR OWN

Spend a few moments meditating on Philippians 4:8. Which of the things mentioned will you purpose to dwell on this week? Write out a brief prayer, asking God to help you focus your mind there.

PRAYER TIME

End your time together by taking prayer requests related to the topics in this session's study. Call on a person to pray for your group.

INTRODUCTION

I know now why my mom never went to bed early on Friday and Saturday nights when I was a teenager. It was only after I had returned home for the evening safe and sound that she could nestle into her bed and drift off to sleep.

I can remember walking in the front door and seeing her sitting on our sofa dressed in her pajamas and fuzzy bathrobe, hair curled up for the night. She wasn't sleeping. She might have been watching television. Or perhaps reading a book. But usually, she was sipping black coffee and looking out our big picture window, waiting for the car lights to slice through the darkness, signaling my return home.

Back then, I found it unusual and unnecessary. As a teenager, I treasured my sleep. If I were tuckered out, there wasn't much that could keep me from crawling under my covers and drifting off to la-la land, sometimes until noon the next day! Besides, why did she need to stay awake? I always returned home safely before whatever time she'd told me to be there. I knew there was always the possibility of an emergency. However, if that did happen, she would hear the phone ring, waking her from her slumber.

Fast forward a couple of decades.

Now I get it. As life marches on, our roles and responsibilities change. We may become a spouse. Or a parent. Our career may connect us with people whom we love. We accumulate possessions or property, which we are responsible to pay for and maintain. These added layers to life—which we didn't have as a teenager—all bring about a boatload of reasons to worry. I have spent many nights sitting up late, waiting for my own teenagers to return home or wondering how we were going to make a certain payment on time.

Yes, life provides many opportunities to worry. But what does worry accomplish? It seems it only makes us lose sleep and gain gray hairs. What does the Bible say about worry? Is there a way we can take our anxious feelings and do something productive with them? Let's dive into the final chapter of Philippians to discover just what to do when we are tempted to wring our hands in fear of what might happen next.

READ IT CAREFULLY

We are nearing the homestretch in our study of Philippians. This session, we are zeroing in on the first nine verses of this final chapter. Read through this segment of Scripture in one sitting or at least over the course of one day. Once you have finished, re-read it again leisurely. As you do, note the verses that jump out at you and why. Is it because you have a question about that particular verse or passage of Scripture? Does the content encourage you as you face a current situation? Does it convict, inspire, or challenge you? Record the verses that stand out, as well as your reasons for choosing them.

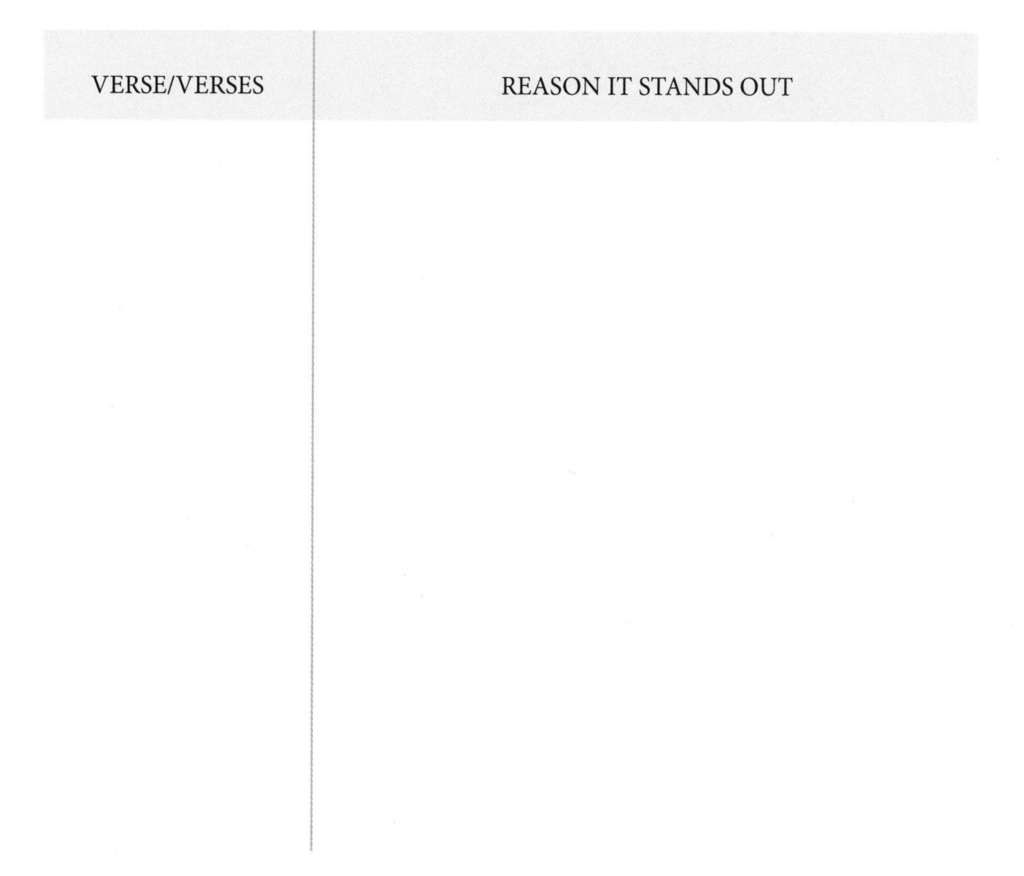

VERSE/VERSES	REASON IT STANDS OUT

Now, go back and place a star beside the verse that most encouraged or challenged you in the text. Then put a question mark beside the one that most puzzled you.

Continue your running list of the topics covered in Philippians. Jot down any topics mentioned in 4:1-9 along with the corresponding verse reference.

TOPIC	VERSE WHERE IT IS FOUND

Now that you have read these verses carefully, answer the following questions:

Did you discover anything new in this passage you had not noticed in the Bible before? If so, record it here.

Did you spy an old familiar verse in this passage anywhere? If so, which one?

Did you notice any interesting topic covered in this passage you didn't know the Bible covered? If so, what topic?

Good work! Now, spend a little time praying that God will help you internalize this chunk of Scripture and maximize your study of it in the next section as we cover it more in-depth.

STUDY IT PRAYERFULLY

Now that you've vigilantly read the verses for this week, let's dive in to extract the meaning and ascertain some everyday life lessons.

STANDING FIRM

The first verse of this final chapter is a commentary and a commission based on the previous chapter, which we studied in our last lesson. As Paul urged his readers to reach forward to God's goal, he buttoned up his pep talk by expressing his love for the Philippians—referring to them as his joy and crown—and then gave them this admonition: stand firm.

In our English translation this charge to the Philippians is presented in two words, but in the original Greek language, it was just one word. This word is also used in the following verses found elsewhere in Scripture. Read the verses, and record insights into what it means to stand firm. Also note the times when we need to.

VERSE	INSIGHTS
Romans 14:4	
1 Corinthians 16:13	
Galatians 5:1	
1 Thessalonians 3:8	
2 Thessalonians 2:15	

Now that you have looked over these Scriptures, write a definition of what you think it means to stand firm.

The Greek meaning of this phrase is *to hold fast* or *to persevere*. Look up the word *persevere*. What does it mean?

Has there ever been a time in your faith walk when you needed to stand firm and persevere despite the opposition you were facing? If so, briefly describe it.

Based on what we've studied so far in this letter, why do you think Paul felt it necessary to urge the Philippian church to stand firm and persevere in their faith?

CHRISTIAN CONFLICTS

Paul switched gears in verses 2 and 3 and mentioned by name two women in the church: Euodia and Syntyche. (Pronounced "yoo-oo'-diah" and "sin'-tah-chee" in case you'd like to wow your group sometime while reading this passage out loud!) Euodia's name means either sweet fragrance or prosperous journey. Scholars aren't exactly sure. Syntyche means with fate or fortunate.

It seems that there had been a little kerfuffle between these two women in the Philippian church. So Paul asked another person, referred to as the "true partner" (CSB) or "true companion" (NIV) in verse 3, to help these women smooth out the differences between them. Some researchers say that this unidentified church member was perhaps Silas or Timothy. Still others believe that it was Epaphroditus, the bearer of the letter. Whoever the person, they were given the task of helping these women to reconcile their relationship.

At the very least, this passage teaches us this important fact: sometimes Christians experience conflict, even those who have labored side by side for the cause of Christ. Paul mentioned in verse 3 that the women had worked alongside him for the sake of the gospel. He also didn't question the authenticity of either woman's faith because he referred to them as having their names "in the book of life."

The book of life is the heavenly record written by God before the foundation of the earth. It is mentioned in both the Old Testament (Ex. 32:32; Ps. 69:28; Dan. 12:1) and the New Testament (Luke 10:20; Heb. 12:23; Rev. 17:8; 21:27). This book contains the names of all true believers, those who have placed their faith in Christ and been born into God's family. The unrighteous will have their names erased or blotted out.

Have you ever experienced conflict between yourself and another Christian or observed conflict between two other believers whom you know personally? Describe the situation briefly in the space provided.

Look up the following verses. What does each passage tell you about conflict between believers? In the chart below, record any helpful phrases or concepts you discover about what we should—or should not do—when facing disagreements.

VERSE	WHAT TO DO	WHAT NOT TO DO
Proverbs 17:14		
Matthew 5:25		
Luke 12:58		
Luke 17:3-4		
Acts 15:36-40		
Romans 14:19		
Romans 15:5		
Ephesians 4:3		

Colossians 3:13		
2 Timothy 2:14		

After gleaning guidance from the previous Scriptures, write out a two- or three-sentence goal or plan for how you will move forward the next time you experience conflict with another Christian.

The next time I experience conflict with another Christian, I will:

ON JOY AND GENTLENESS

As a child, do you remember your mom or dad telling you to do something—like take out the trash or stop bickering with your sibling—and then for emphasis add, "And don't make me say it again"? Yeah. Me too.

In this passage "father" Paul is assuming his spiritual children need him to repeat himself, and so he doesn't simply urge them to, "Rejoice in the Lord" and then move on to the next topic. Nope. He implores them to, "Rejoice in the Lord always" (v. 4). And then for additional impact he adds, "I will say it again: Rejoice!" (v. 4).

Paul had already encouraged his flock at Philippi to rejoice in the Lord at the beginning of chapter 3.

Why do you think Paul needed to address joy again as he neared the end of this letter? What have you learned the Philippian church was dealing with that might necessitate a focus on rejoicing in the Lord?

In difficult circumstances, do you sometimes need to remind yourself to focus on rejoicing in the Lord? At such times, what verse, phrase, or sentence can you repeat in your mind to help you recalculate your thoughts, seeking to dwell in the joy of the Lord?

In verse 5, what specific character quality did Paul want the Philippians to display broadly.

This quality of *graciousness* (or *gentleness* in some translations) in the Greek language meant mild, fair, forbearing, and reasonable. This is not the only place this word appears in the Bible.

Flip or tap your way to the following verses where either this exact word or similar concept is used. After each reference, jot down any additional thoughts that give you a clearer picture of what graciousness/gentleness looks like in the life of a believer.
Proverbs 15:1

Colossians 4:5-6

1 Timothy 3:3

Titus 3:2

James 3:17

1 Peter 2:18

Immediately following Paul's instructions that the Philippians let their gentleness be known to everyone, he makes this statement: "The Lord is near." *The Lord is near.*

Near, in this case, could refer to both time and proximity. The early church felt that the time for Jesus to return was very soon, definitely within their lifetime. This may have been what Paul was pointing to. However, Paul could also have been reminding them of God's constant presence. When we are facing troubles, we need to remember this important truth. Although we may not sense His presence all the time, nevertheless, the Lord is near.

How can the Lord be near to where we currently dwell? Through the miracle of the Holy Spirit. He lives within us. He sees our situation. He knows our pain and suffering. He observes our rejoicing. He knows the deepest desires of our hearts.

How often do you earnestly feel the Lord near to you as you go about your day? Place an X on the continuum below that shows your answer.

Never   Rarely   Sometimes   Often   Daily

Now think about your answer. If you placed your X somewhere between "never" and "sometimes," why do you think you have a hard time believing the Lord is near?

If, instead, your X landed somewhere between "sometimes" and "always," what helps you believe the truth of this verse, that God is near to you?

Regardless of where you placed your X, let's meander through the Book of Psalms for a few minutes, discovering more about God being near. Read over the following verses slowly, soaking in the deep truths you notice.

- □ Psalm 34:18
- □ Psalm 73:28
- □ Psalm 119:151
- □ Psalm 145:18

Was there a specific verse you feel could inspire you during those times where you don't sense God being close by? If so, circle it. I encourage you to commit this verse to memory and write it down on a note card to keep in your Bible for those days when you need it.

Worry is like a rocking chair: it keeps you moving but doesn't get you anywhere.

CORRIE TEN BOOM[1]

OUSTING ANXIETY

I inherited many things from my mother. Her aqua blue eyes. Her love of cooking. And unfortunately, her tendency to worry. When one of my teenagers or adult children is late to return home, my mind goes to all sorts of awful scenarios. By the time they finally walk through the door, twenty minutes later than expected, I have their entire funeral planned out.

It isn't just my darling offspring that I worry about. I have also been known to worry about money. And health issues. I worry that what I said may have offended someone and now I am facing a possibly fractured friendship. I worry that I'm not doing enough at church. Or I worry that I'm doing too much and it may affect my emotional stability. It seems I never run out of people or things to worry about.

Read Philippians 4:6-7 (NIV). Then, fill in the missing words in the following paragraph.

Do not be __________ about ______________, but in __________ situation, by ______________ and ________________, with ___________________, present your requests to God. And the __________ of God, which _______________ all understanding, will guard your __________ and your __________ in Christ Jesus.

Of all the words you placed in the blanks above, circle one that is particularly meaningful to you today. Briefly explain why you chose that word.

After the apostle Paul stated not to be anxious and worried, he told us what to do instead: "in every situation, by prayer and petition, with thanksgiving, present your requests to God" (Phil. 4:6, NIV).

I remember the first time I read Philippians 4:6-7 when I was in high school. I thought it was rather peculiar that it mentioned prayers, petitions, and requests. I wondered how these three words were different.

It turns out that a different Greek word is used for each one. The one we translate as *petitions* or *supplications* means to ask for something you lack or entreating God due to a deep personal need. The word translated *prayers* speaks more of a prayer exchange—one where we are presenting requests to God but where we also hear from Him. It can also mean a physical place of prayer. Sometimes the word was used to denote a location of prayer for the Jews when no synagogue was nearby. Finally, the word *requests* meant more of a petition. A *petition* is defined as a formal plea, typically one signed by many people, appealing to authority with respect to a particular cause.

There are so many things in our lives that can cause us to be anxious—relationships, job situations, finances, church, and the list goes on. And when difficulties arise, our first reaction is to worry. But it doesn't have to be. When you feel the worry rising, don't entertain the anxious thoughts. Be intentional about immediately choosing prayer. Make this a consistent practice. Let's start now.

Use the space provided to list three things you're currently anxious about. Then use a different colored pen or marker to write over them "I will not worry. I will pray." Then spend a few moments presenting these concerns to the Lord.

1.

2.

3.

Note how we are to present our prayers, petitions, and supplications to God according to verse 6.

We are to present them with ________________________.

Did you catch it? We are supposed to turn our anxious thoughts into prayer requests, presented with the attitude of thanksgiving in our hearts and on our lips.

Why is presenting our requests with thanksgiving so important?

You may wonder how it would be possible to be thankful in situations that are causing such deep anxiety. In those times you can thank God for His sovereignty. Thank God for His presence. Thank Him for hearing your prayers and being faithful to answer. Gratefulness can turn our worry into worship, which takes the focus off of our needs and instead places it on God's sufficiency in our situation.

Have you ever experienced a time in your life when you turned your worry into worship? If so, what happened?

Since we are supposed to make our requests with thanksgiving, let's explore verses that have to do with thanksgiving. Read the following passages, then choose one to use this week to wrap your prayers in a cushion of thanksgiving as you make your requests to God.

- □ Psalm 34:1
- □ Psalm 92:1-2
- □ Psalm 119:62
- □ Colossians 3:17
- □ Colossians 4:2
- □ Hebrews 12:28

Perhaps right now you're worried or anxious about something—a relationship, a situation at work, finances, and so forth.

Take a moment to pray, presenting your requests to God with thanksgiving. Feel free to write your prayer in the space provided.

For the next week, whenever you feel anxiety welling up inside of you, turn to thankfulness. Either out loud or in your mind, whisper a prayer of thankfulness to God. Name five things you are grateful for related to your situation. Stop letting your mind migrate to a place of worry. Instead, purpose to be a person of thankfulness, turning your worry into worship.

PRACTICING PEACE

When we turn our worry into prayers surrounded by gratefulness, we are promised peace. But not just your plain, garden variety type of peace. We are promised peace that passes all understanding (Phil. 4:7).

This indescribable peace we experience through Christ will guard both our hearts and minds. The word for heart is *kardia*. It's easy to see a correlation to modern-day words that have to do with the heart such as cardiology or cardiac. *Kardia* is defined as the inner self, the center of your will and intention. The word for mind is *noēma,* and it means the center of thought. It is closely related to another word for mind that is defined as the outcome of the thought process, the verdict you pronounce after you have mulled something over in your brain.

Isn't this utterly astonishing? God's Word promises to give us a peace that will protect us from the runaway emotions flooding our hearts and the racing thoughts ricocheting through our minds when we face an anxious situation.

What else can we learn about the peace of Christ? Read the following verses, and fill in the blanks.

Isaiah 26:3—God will keep your mind in __________ peace because you _______________ in Him.

John 14:27—This peace is not like the peace of _________. It keeps our hearts from being __________ or __________.

Romans 5:1—We have been declared righteous through faith and have peace with God through _______ _______ ___________ ____________.

Colossians 3:15—The peace of Christ should _________ our hearts.

WHERE TO PARK OUR MINDS

I tease my husband sometimes when I see him with a certain look on his face. He could be sitting with me at the fire pit in our backyard, staring at the crackling flames. Or when he's looking out the window of our vehicle while I am driving. No matter the place, the look is the same. I will often say to him, "What are you thinking?" to which he will reply, "Nothing." What?

Nothing? How can a person be thinking nothing? I don't ever think in all my days I have ever thought nothing at any given time—unless I was asleep! And I always tell him the same thing each time he answers me this way: "I am so jealous! I wish I knew how to think nothing!"

You see, most days my mind gives me fits. It can concoct scenarios that are not true. It jumps to conclusions that are not so. It often assumes the worst rather than believes the best. Sometimes at night, I simply cannot shut my mind down. It roars and races and causes me to get all worked up. My mind simply doesn't know how to idle in neutral—as my husband's does—nor does it know how to think on the right things.

Philippians 4:8 gives us a thought list of where we need to park our minds. Instead of idling in anxiety, we are to think on several magnificent things. List them in the space provided.

Whatever is:

1.

2.

3.

4.

5.

6.

7.

8.

Which one of these eight items are the easiest for you to think about?

Which one of these is the most difficult for you to dwell on?

Finally, which one do you need most to contemplate at this point in your life? Explain.

Write out a one-sentence prayer to God, asking Him to empower you to think on the one thing you most need to contemplate.

LIVE IT OUT PRACTICALLY

Congratulations on your diligent study this week of the first half of Philippians 4. We've examined what to do during times of conflict with other Christians. We've covered joy, gentleness, and how to sense the nearness of the Lord. Our study covered the topic of worry and what to do when we feel anxiousness welling up inside of us. Lastly, we have pondered what we should ponder. Time now to live out some of what we have discovered.

THE EXCEPTIONAL EIGHT

Philippians 4:8 gives us eight "dwell on these things" instructions. These are the types of thought we are to allow to dance into our minds and take root. Things that are:

- True
- Honorable
- Just
- Pure
- Lovely
- Commendable
- Excellent
- Praiseworthy

Dwell on these things!

To truly ponder these "exceptional eight," we need to learn to flip the script. When our minds start to wander down a wrong path, we must interrupt those thoughts, take them captive, and replace them with the type of thoughts Paul urges us to have in this passage. Just what do I mean? Here is one example for you.

When my mind entertains thoughts that tempt me to believe I have sinned so often or so grievously God does not love me anymore, I intentionally turn my thoughts to think on that which is true (number one in the list of the exceptional eight). This is what is true: Nothing can ever separate me from the love of God that is mine in Christ Jesus. This truth is based on Romans 8:38-39:

> *For I am persuaded that neither death nor life, nor angels nor rulers, nor things present nor things to come, nor powers, nor height nor depth, nor any other created thing will be able to separate us from the love of God that is in Christ Jesus our Lord.*

Prayer: Father help me to remember that nothing can separate me from Your love. Although I still sin and need to come to You in repentance, You are faithful and just to forgive my sin and cleanse me from all unrighteousness (1 John 1:9). You never withdraw Your love from a believer. Thank You for this powerful truth. Help me walk in confidence today, knowing You love and care for me immensely. In Jesus' name, amen.

Now it's your turn. Using the template below, fill in your own example of something you are currently facing. Use a concordance or online search tools such as BibleGateway.com to locate a relevant verse. Then replace the wrong thinking in your mind with the truth of one of the exceptional eight characteristics, coupled with the powerful Scripture that applies to your particular situation.

When my mind entertains thoughts that tempt me to believe:

I, instead, need to think on that which is ____________. (Number ______ in the list of the exceptional eight.)

A verse that will help me in this endeavor is _________________, that reads:

My Prayer:

CHALLENGE OF THE WEEK

Take advantage of the opportunity to put into practice the scriptural lessons you've learned this week by choosing to complete one of the following challenges. Be prepared to tell your group the outcome of your activity.

1. **ANSWER WITH GENTLENESS.** Philippians 4:5 tells us to let our gentleness be known to everyone. Sometimes the hardest people to be gentle with are those with whom we have the most contact. Probably for most of us that's the people who live under our roofs. For others it could be the coworkers you see every day at your job.

   Showing gentleness is often most difficult when engaging in conversation with those people. For me, it is especially difficult to be gracious with people who ask me the same question over and over again. Or with those who ask me a question I think they should already know the answer to. Proverbs 15:1 states, "A gentle answer turns away anger, but a harsh word stirs up wrath." Make it your goal this week to answer everyone in a gentle way, even if they seem to be acting in a harsh manner toward you. Commit to not throwing more fuel on the fire but deflecting the anger by giving gentle answers. See if weaving gentleness into your words and demeanor this week brings about any beneficial changes in your relationships with those closest to you.

2. **GO ON A GRATITUDE EXCURSION.** As soon as you rise each morning this week and each evening right before you go to sleep, write down in a journal—or on a notes app on your phone—five things for which you are grateful. See if adopting this habit helps you to turn your worry into worship.

3. **START DOWN THE RECONCILIATION ROAD.** Have you had a conflict with another Christian similar to the one Euodia and Syntyche experienced? Determine to reach out to that person this week to initiate a conversation leading to forgiveness and perhaps even reconciliation. It may be hard, but it is in keeping with the Bible's instructions for us found in Matthew 18:21; Luke 17:4; and Ephesians 4:32. Perhaps reading these verses before reaching out to that person will help give you confidence in approaching him or her and provide appropriate words to say.

MEMORY VERSE

OPTIONAL MEMORY VERSE

Remember that for each lesson, there is an optional memory verse provided to help you further internalize the message of the passages we studied together. To assist you in this endeavor, all six passages are printed in the back of the study guide.

You may want to see if someone else in your group would like to come early or stay a few minutes after your group time so the two of you can practice saying the verses out loud to each other.

This session's verse is a template for turning our worry into worship, thanking God, and experiencing His indescribable peace.

Don't worry about anything, but in everything, through prayer
and petition with thanksgiving, present your requests to God.
And the peace of God, which surpasses all understanding,
will guard your hearts and minds in Christ Jesus.
PHILIPPIANS 4:6-7

Don't worry about anything, but in everything, through prayer and petition with thanksgiving, present your requests to God. And the peace of God, which surpasses all understanding, will guard your hearts and minds in Christ Jesus.

PHILIPPIANS 4:6-7

WEEK 6

WHAT MATTERS MOST

CHASING CONTENTMENT

I have learned to be content in whatever circumstances I find myself. I know both how to make do with little, and I know how to make do with a lot. In any and all circumstances I have learned the secret of being content—whether well fed or hungry, whether in abundance or in need. I am able to do all things through him who strengthens me.

PHILIPPIANS 4:11b-13

VIEWER GUIDE

FAVORITE QUOTES

STAND-OUT SCRIPTURES

GROUP GUIDE

ICEBREAKER

What social media platforms do you use? How has social media affected your contentment? Have you ever experienced the feeling of coming apart at the "seems" when you spied someone on social media who seems to have a better life than you?

1. *Karen made the following statement:* Often those who are most content are the ones who have the least. *Do you agree? Why or why not? Do you have any real-life examples that reflect this statement?*

2. *Karen said her mom gave this advice for whenever you feel down on your circumstances:* Remember that there is always someone out there who has it worse off than you. Go find that person and make their day. Somehow it will make yours as well. *Have you ever found this to be true? What happened?*

3. *Karen stated that the definition of contentment is "to be satisfied to the point where I am no longer disturbed or disquieted." How does that help you in your understanding of biblical contentment?*

4. *Paul said he had learned the secret of contentment (v. 12), which means it was a process, a skill he needed to acquire. What has helped you to learn to be content?*

5. *Review Philippians 4:13. How have you seen this verse misused? Have you ever been guilty of misusing it? Explain*

6. *How would you explain the meaning of Philippians 4:13 to a new believer? How does the context of verses 11-12 clarify the meaning?*

7. *Paul commended the Philippian church for being so eager to meet his needs. Do you see your church acting in similar ways to meet people's needs? Explain. If so, how are you involved? If not, how can you help initiate this kind of ministry?*

8. *How has God fulfilled the promise of Philippians 4:19 in your life?*

ON YOUR OWN

Contentment isn't just having what you want. It is wanting nothing more than what you already have. Take a few moments to write out a short prayer to God, thanking Him for the many things you already possess.

PRAYER TIME

Close out your time together by sharing prayer requests related to the topics in this session's study. Then, call on one person to close out your time together in prayer.

INTRODUCTION

When I was a little girl, an elderly woman lived a few houses down from us. We called her Grandma Hoffman. She was a mentor to my mother and a kind soul to everyone she met. She taught my mom to recognize the difference between a flower and a weed. She let us neighborhood kids pick apples in her backyard. She taught me to put milk in my tomato soup. When I moved away to college, she'd clip and send me encouraging magazine articles or slips of paper with Scripture scrawled on it.

There came a day when Grandma Hoffman, then a widow, had to move from her home. She left her large yard full of flowers, vegetable gardens, and a grove of fruit trees for a tiny one-room studio apartment in a high-rise building for seniors. While this might make others sad, it didn't seem to change her demeanor. Although she had little furniture, sparse décor, and just a half dozen or so dresses, Grandma never complained. She was always so grateful, so cheerful. Her greatest joys were the people in her life and her relationship with God.

By the time I got married, Grandma Hoffman was on a walker, struggling to get around. But she was at the wedding. When my husband and I opened our wedding cards that day, many times we found a high-dollar check. But when we opened Grandma Hoffman's card, out fell a wrinkled five-dollar bill. It was my very favorite wedding gift because I knew the sacrifice she made to give it.

But perhaps the most treasured item she ever gave me was a tiny piece of paper that contained the typewritten words of Isaiah 40:8: "The grass withers, the flowers fade, but the word of our God remains forever." Underneath the verse she had written in her shaky, cursive handwriting, "Isn't it grand to know?"

In this session we will tackle the topic of chasing contentment. A quick peek at social media will show us what most people long for in their search for happiness—romance, money, position, possessions, or popularity. But do these things usher us into a life of contentment? If that's the case, then why do so many who have so much end up so miserable? And how can a simple widow whose possessions would fit in the back of a pick-up truck and whose bank account was barely existent, be so joyful and at peace with her lot in life? What did Grandma Hoffman know that many others don't?

Perhaps the answer is found in the Bible verse she sent me. When I read that tiny piece of paper that I've carried for almost forty years, I can say, "Yes, Grandma Hoffman. Yes!" So many things I've tried to put my trust in have eventually faded away. People change. Relationships wither. Our financial situation shifts. We change careers, homes, and roles over the years. But the one thing that never fades, changes, nor fails to bring life, is the holy Word of God.

Let's study this life-giving Word together as Paul shares the secret of contentment.

READ IT CAREFULLY

Let's finish our hike through Philippians by reading 4:10-23. Read this portion of Scripture in one sitting or at least over the course of one day. Once you have finished, go back and marinate in these verses, reading them unhurriedly. As you do, note the verses that jump out at you and why. Is it because you have a question about that particular verse or segment of Scripture? Does the content encourage you as you face a current situation? Does it convict, inspire, or challenge you? Record the verses that stand out, as well as your reasons for choosing them, in the spaces provided.

VERSE/VERSES	REASON IT STANDS OUT

Now, go back and place a star beside the verse that most encouraged or challenged you in the text. Then, put a question mark beside the one that most puzzled you.

Continue your running list of the topics covered in Philippians. Chronicle any subjects mentioned in 4:10-23 along with the corresponding verse reference.

TOPIC	VERSE WHERE IT IS FOUND

Now that you have read these verses carefully, answer the following questions:

Did you discover anything new in this passage you had not noticed in the Bible before? If so, record it here.

Did you spy an old familiar verse in this passage anywhere? If so, which one?

Did you notice any interesting topic covered in this passage you didn't know the Bible covered? If so, what topic?

Great job! Now, spend some time praying that God will speak to you through these final verses of Philippians and amplify your study of it as we cover it more thoroughly.

STUDY IT PRAYERFULLY

Now that you've carefully read this final portion of Paul's letter, it is time to investigate it verse-by-verse to unearth the meaning and uncover some real-world application.

UNLOCKING THE SECRET TO CONTENTMENT

Over my years as an adult, I have observed many people. I've found when it comes to feeling content with their lot in life, people fall into two different categories.

Some seem restless, feeling their life situations are lacking. They may exhibit feelings of jealousy as they talk about others in their lives. "Must be nice" often rolls off their lips—or at least dances through their minds—as they observe those who seem to have more romantic marriages, bigger homes, more successful careers, or better behaved children, Their wish list doesn't have to be anything monetary or relational. It could relate to physical looks, personal achievements, or more exciting experiences.

The second category of people seem settled in their souls when it comes to contentment. They don't seem to be chasing the elusive state of blissfulness they can't quite seem to snag. They seemed content with their circumstances, their homes, their things, and their relationships. Their contentment seems to give them a sense of calm and feeling of confidence knowing that what they have is enough.

And here's the funny thing, it isn't that people in the second group are better off financially or have higher, more prestigious positions in society. In fact, usually the opposite is true—those who have less in life sometimes possess more contentment. This has been especially true of people I've observed who live in a developing country. Often I saw the deepest joy in the lives of those who were living in the deepest poverty. How can this be?

Paul made a very bold statement in these final verses of Philippians: "I have learned the secret of being content" (4:12). What could that secret be? Our final study together will help us unlock that secret and apply it to our lives in a way that empowers us to cultivate contentment as well.

THANK YOU FOR YOUR SUPPORT

This section of Philippians begins with Paul telling his friends how joyful he is that once again they have "renewed their care" for him (v. 10). Remember that this infant church had sent support by way of Epaphroditus (2:25).

Look carefully at verse 10. What (or who) was the object of Paul's joy in this situation?

In what other verses in Philippians have you seen the topic of rejoicing in the Lord?

It is true that people can perform actions and give gifts that make us joyful. However, there is something special about receiving love and assistance from a Christian brother or sister that makes us not only thankful to them but causes us to rejoice in the Lord.

Can you think of a time when a fellow Christian provided for your needs, causing you to feel immense gratitude toward God and joy in Him? Describe it.

Verse 10 also mentions that the Philippian church was concerned for Paul's well-being and life situation, yet lacked the opportunity to show him their care.

Has there ever been a time when you wanted to help out a fellow Christian but, for one reason or another, you were unable to? What happened?

Check out the verses below, all of which talk about caring for fellow Christians. Once you've read them carefully, write a sentence or two describing the care that should take place between fellow believers.
Romans 12:10

Galatians 6:2

Galatians 6:10

Hebrews 6:10

James 2:14-17

On a scale of 1 to 10, with 1 being *totally oblivious* and 10 being *keenly in-tune*, how mindful are you to the needs of fellow Christians, both locally and globally?

Totally Oblivious									*Keenly In-tune*
1	2	3	4	5	6	7	8	9	10

Considering your score, would you say that your awareness usually leads to action? Why or why not?

Take a few moments to list the names of fellow believers, either specific people or groups, who are experiencing financial, physical, or emotional needs. Don't do anything other than list them for now. We will refer back to this section when we issue the challenges for the week.

CULTIVATING CONTENTMENT

Carefully read Philippians 4:11-13. Then answer the following questions. Did Paul say that being content comes naturally or is learned?

What word in verse 11 described the type of circumstances in which Paul learned to be content?

What does the word *whatever* mean? Look it up in a dictionary or an online source.

The CSB version of verse 12 says that Paul knows how to "make do with little" and he knows how to "make do with a lot." What two opposite phrases does your Bible version use?

Think back over your life for a moment. In what period would you say you had to make do with very little? Briefly describe it.

Conversely, at what point in your life did you experience the most abundance? Share a little about that season.

Now consider your level of contentment during those two opposite times. Did you find it easier to be content during the season of abundance or the time of want? Or would you say you were equally content in both situations? If equal, was your level of contentment low or high, like Paul's?

Paul made a very bold statement in the middle of verse 12. He told the Philippian church that he had learned the secret of being content.

What does the word *learned* tell you about Paul's view of contentment?

When we say we learned something, we recognize that the knowledge or skill we've gained is not something we were born with. It's been acquired. Paul lived through many seasons of life that put him in all sorts of circumstances. He was once well-known and looked up to as a Pharisee. He was both feared by Christians and revered by Jews. He had riches. But he also had times of sorrow and periods of financial trouble. He was in prison and falsely accused.

How do you think these many different situations helped Paul unlock the secret of being content?

Let's consider for a moment why we don't experience contentment in life. I think one of the top reasons is best illustrated by introducing you to one of my favorite people.

Five-year-old Ryan was our next-door neighbor. This blond-haired, brown-eyed spitfire's favorite pastime was riding his bike. His rickety, red girl's Schwinn® bicycle had been handed down through several cousins before making its way into Ryan's garage—and into his heart.

It didn't matter to Ryan that it was badly in need of repair. He proudly paraded that contraption up and down our block each afternoon. So, imagine my surprise when one September day, I happened upon Ryan kicking his beloved bike as it lay on the ground.

"What are you doing, buddy?" I questioned.

"Stupid bike," he murmured still striking it with the toe of his tennis shoe. "Cool kids have a bright blue, Mudpuppy dirt bike, not some dumb old girl's bike from their cousin." This greatly perplexed me since I knew how much he cherished that bike.

And then it dawned on me what day it was—Ryan's first day of kindergarten. And sure enough, at recess the kids discussed what bikes they owned. In Ryan's eyes his prized possession had suddenly turned stupid. His contentment had vanished. Why?

Comparisons. Comparisons kill contentment. Is that not totally true?

My home is just fine—until a coworker builds one that is larger or more functional—you know with all those cool roll-out cupboards and organizational storage. My furniture and comforters are completely satisfactory. That is until I wander into Pottery Barn®. Nothing wrong with my car. Until I carpooled with Claire. She has a brand-new Cadillac—with some super sweet cup holders! (I know cars boast many amazing features, but it's the cup holders that help me make my choice.)

And my kids? Oh, I love my kids. Those sweet, sometimes argumentative, but mostly charming children. Until I think of an acquaintance at church who has seemingly perfect, obedient offspring who utter "yes, ma'am" and "no, sir" on cue, and whose personalities don't get under my skin or on my nerves like my dear darlings' do.

You see, we are usually content with our own old, red Schwinn hand-me-down, until we spy someone else on her new bright blue Mudpuppy.

Generations of people have struggled with letting comparisons kill their contentment. It's the old "keeping up with the Joneses" syndrome. However, something has changed in our society. It is the amount of time we spend spying the Joneses. In my parents' and grandparents' day, you only saw the Jones family once or twice a week, perhaps at church or the PTA meeting at school. But now the Joneses parade in front of our eyes all day long. Where?

On social media.

You notice a friend post a picture of a romantic and expensive dinner with her husband while you're eating leftovers and having a spat with your spouse. Or you happen upon a post about your friend's child winning "Student of the Month" at the local middle school while your middle schooler sits busted in the principal's office. He and his buddies pulled a prank they found completely hilarious but which the substitute teacher found no humor in. (Not that it's ever happened to anyone I know! Gulp.)

I recently conducted an online poll of my followers on social media. I asked them to list various areas in which they found it difficult to be content due to comparisons made on social media. Among the topics they listed were financial situations, marriage, behavior and accomplishments of children, houses, possessions, friendships, and—coming in number one—their looks, especially when it comes to their weight. Of those polled, a resounding 97.5% of them said it was difficult for them to look at the social media accounts of others without feeling at least a little bit of jealousy, which leads to feeling discontent.

> So what is our solution to this dilemma? It's found in verse 13. But not in the way you may have seen verse 13 utilized before.

Philippians 4:13 tends to be a familiar and frequently quoted passage of Scripture in Christian circles. However, it seems that often we almost peel this promise from off the page. We take it out of the context of learning to be content and how Christ empowers us to do so, and slap it on many other situations, like a money-back guarantee.

Worried you can't pass the entrance exam? Just tell yourself, "I am able to do all things through Him who strengthens me."

Need to drop a few pounds and so you are starting a diet on Monday morning? While you are munching on your kale chips, between bites, repeat out loud, "I am able to do all things through Him who strengthens me."

But was this verse really meant to be a magic bullet for all life's situations?

Let's look at this verse in a different manner. We can still apply it to multiple situations, but not as a guarantee of a positive outcome. Instead let's see it as Christ's strength helping us settle into a place of contentment, despite the outcome of our situation.

The secret is Christ in me, not me in a different set of circumstances.

ELISABETH ELLIOT[1]

We can learn to be content, no matter if we pass or fail the entrance exam. We can learn to discover contentment no matter what the scale says. This doesn't mean we just give up and use contentment as an excuse to cop out, failing to pursue excellence. However, this verse is also not a panacea that we slap on a situation to usher in success. It is an attitude perspective we maintain despite our situation. It is realizing the truth found in a quote by one of my all-time favorite Christian female authors, Elisabeth Elliot, who declared this:

> *The secret is Christ in me, not me in a different set of circumstances.[2]*

I hope that quote snapped you to reality like it did me when I first read it nearly two decades ago.

Let's look for a moment at some verses that talk about Christ in us. Read the following Scripture passages. After each one, jot down any phrases or words that jump out at you. Also put a star next to your two or three favorite ones.

Romans 8:10

1 Corinthians 6:17

2 Corinthians 4:6-7

Galatians 2:20

Galatians 4:19

Ephesians 3:16-19

Colossians 1:27

Colossians 3:1-3

1 John 3:1-2

The secret to being content is an eternal mind-set; a thought process that realizes all the trinkets and treasures and the possessions and positions here on earth are temporary. The only thing that lasts is our position in Christ and His Spirit living in us.

Why is it hard to maintain this eternal mind-set in our culture?

Which of the areas listed below do you have the hardest time finding contentment in? Mark it.

- Looks
- Financial situation
- Marriage
- Behavior and accomplishments of children
- House
- Health
- Possessions
- Friendships
- Extended family relationships
- Employment situation or status as a stay-at-home parent
- Other ____________________ (fill in the blank with your own)

Now, go back and read again the verses you starred earlier. How do they help you shift your perspective about the area you marked above?

Write the verse(s) in your own words in the space provided. Circle any key words or phrases that help in altering your outlook.

The word that is rendered *content* in this passage literally means to be satisfied to the point where I am no longer disturbed or disquieted. What a remarkable picture! It reminds me of a tired and restless child who finally falls asleep in the arms of her mother. Satisfied. No longer disturbed. No longer disquieted.

That's the place God has already prepared for us in the midst of life's storms. He is longing for us to take our eyes off our situation—or off another person—and fix them solely upon Him.

TAKING IT PERSONALLY

Reread Paul's words about his personal life situation in Philippians 4:11-13. They are written out for you here in the CSB version:

> *I have learned to be content in whatever circumstances I find myself. I know both how to make do with little, and I know how to make do with a lot. In any and all circumstances I have learned the secret of being content—whether well fed or hungry, whether in abundance or in need. I am able to do all things through him who strengthens me.*

Another rendering of this passage could read this way:

> *I have learned to have a quiet and undisturbed heart no matter what type of situation I find myself in. I can be brought low, humiliated, and humbled. Or I can dwell in conditions that exceed my necessities and are in abundance; an overflow of blessings. I am able to prevail in every kind of thing—all the parts that make up the whole—through Jesus Christ who fills me with power and makes me strong.*

This rendering tells us that we are able to prevail, meaning there is something we are fighting against—an enemy, a situation, an obstacle. And we are able to prevail over every single part of what we are facing, whether in situations of plenty or want. We can be victorious—through Jesus Christ who fills us with His might to help us overcome.

Let's take this passage and make it personal. Think of a situation you are currently facing in which you need to prevail in the power of Christ. Using the following exercise, fill in the missing sections to make it personal.

I ______________ (your name) can keep a quiet and undisturbed heart, no matter my situation. I could be in this low situation: ______________ ________________________________ or I could dwell in this condition of abundance: ______________________________. I am able to prevail in the midst of _________________________________ (the situation) through _____________________ who fills me with power and makes me strong.

Now, let's put it in a prayer. Determine from now on to live in a state of contentment despite your circumstances. Craft a brief prayer to God about learning and applying the secret to true contentment.

PARTNERING FOR TRUE PROFIT

In verses 14-20 of chapter 4, Paul wrapped up his letter by speaking again about the Philippians providing financial help when he was experiencing hardship.

But there's a phrase in verse 17 that alludes to something that was of even greater importance to him. Write the phrase in the space provided.

Some versions speak of the "profit" that was increasing in the Philippians account because of their partnership with and kindness to Paul. Others versions use the word *fruit*. In the Greek language the word is *karpos*. Sometimes when it is used in Scripture, it does refer to an actual piece of produce as in the fruit of a vine or tree. In other places, it is used to show a result, deed, action, profit, or gain.

In this instance, most biblical scholars believe the second meaning applies since it was a common expression used in business dealings. It seems Paul was pleased with their behavior and so he recognized them for the kind deed they did for him. But he wanted it known that he was not seeking profit for himself, but profit for their spiritual account. He desired that when they appeared before God in heaven, they would gain the benefit of their virtuous acts toward him (Heb. 6:10).

In verse 18, how does Paul describe the care he received from his friends? Fill in the missing words.

A ____________ offering, an ____________ sacrifice, ____________ to God.

How does this verse further showcase the fact that the Philippians' generous giving was not just for Paul, but also for the Lord and was connected to their faith?

The Bible's admonition to help those in financial and physical need has not changed since the time of Paul's letter to the Philippians. However, sometimes the modern church adopts a "just pull yourself up by your bootstraps" mentality. While Scripture does encourage hard work and providing for your own family, we must be careful to balance this against other verses that instruct us to take care of the poor—especially those who cannot work.

Read the following verses and then write a sentence or two summarizing what you learn about providing for the needs of yourself and your family but also providing for the needs of others who are less fortunate and facing hardship.

Exodus 22:25

Leviticus 19:10

Leviticus 25:35

Psalm 41:1

Luke 14:12-14

Galatians 2:10

2 Thessalonians 3:10

1 Timothy 5:8

James 2:2-4

GOD THE SUPPLIER AND FINAL GOODBYES

In Philippians 4:19-20, Paul points the congregation to God's provision. What does he assert that God will do for them and how will He do it?

When we consider God providing for all our needs, we must remember the word *needs*. It does not say He will provide for all our wants. It doesn't mention Him granting our every wish. It says He will provide for our needs.

From the list of definitions below, circle the one you might guess is the definition of the original Greek word for *needs*. Don't read ahead to see the answer. Just read over the following four choices and choose one.

- □ Sanctified longings
- □ Necessary business
- □ Concerns of the human heart
- □ Physical, emotional, and financial essentials

Well—are you ready for the answer? The answer is "necessary business." Paul says God will supply all we need to properly exist here on earth, going about our business, as He sustains us for the journey. He does this according to His riches in glory in Christ Jesus. So, this implies that God has everything at His disposal, yet He knows what each of us needs—and to what extent. By tailoring what He gives to us according to our unique situations, God is truly lavishing us with the best blessings because they are in keeping with His perfect will and His purposes for us.

How often are your prayers filled with a wish list of wants and desires instead of being focused on asking God to supply only what is in accordance with His exact purpose for your life?

Never | Rarely | Sometimes | Often | Daily

Is it wrong to ask God for wants and desires? Explain. At what point does it become wrong?

Take a look at the following verses that are on the topic of our needs and then answer the question that follows each one.
Psalm 34:10—What do those who seek the Lord lack?

Psalm 84:11—What does God bestow and upon whom?

Proverbs 10:3—What does God promise the righteous? The wicked?

Malachi 3:10—What does God provide when we tithe—giving ten percent of our income to Him?

2 Corinthians 9:8—What will God cause to abound to you and why?

SIGNING OFF

In Philippians 4:21-23, Paul delivers his final greetings to "every saint in Christ Jesus." He sends love and greetings from three groups of people: 1) the brothers who are with him, which would have been the men around him who supported and served him, 2) from "all the saints," referencing the larger circle of believers in the church at Rome, and finally, 3) "those who belong to Caesar's household," which could have included some of Caesar's family, but more likely meant those who were in Caesar's employ. This wasn't just an insignificant closing, it was words of encouragement. Support between believers who were often mistreated and even persecuted at that time was essential to their faith. It's no wonder he covered all his bases in this final goodbye!

Do you know of believers—even if they aren't super close to you—who are facing a rough time due to their faith? If so, take some time to send them a personal greeting, either handwritten or online, or at least stop and pray for them as they face their time of trouble.

LIVE IT OUT PRACTICALLY

PIVOT TO PRAISE

Glance over Philippians 4:19-20 again, where Paul wove together our needs with God's provision, then quickly transitioned to worship. With confidence, he told his friends that God would supply not just some of their needs, but all of their needs. He credited Jesus Christ as the source of those abundant gifts, then pivoted to praise by saying, "Now to our God and Father be glory forever and ever. Amen."

Where in your life do you need to pivot to praise? Rather than focusing on what it is that you lack, focus on the Father, who lacks nothing and who can do immeasurably more than you could ever ask or think (Eph. 3:20). Following my example, briefly reference your need in the first column, then pivot to praise by writing a prayer based on an attribute of God. I've given you a list of God's character qualities to help you craft your response.

GOD'S ATTRIBUTES:

- ☐ Good
- ☐ Just
- ☐ Loving
- ☐ Eternal
- ☐ Sovereign
- ☐ Holy
- ☐ Perfect
- ☐ Forgiving
- ☐ Strong
- ☐ Wise
- ☐ Gracious
- ☐ Righteous
- ☐ Slow to anger
- ☐ Protective
- ☐ Faithful
- ☐ Merciful
- ☐ Omnipotent (All-powerful)
- ☐ Omnipresent (Ever-near)
- ☐ Omniscient (All-knowing)

PIVOT TO PRAISE

MY NEED	GOD'S ATTRIBUTE
Direction for our child entering college	*Father, You are omniscient. You know the future, and You know what is best for our child. I will praise You as we place our trust in You each step of the journey, knowing that You alone hold the answers for the questions of her future. Thank You in advance for working everything out according to Your will. In Jesus' name, Amen.*

CHALLENGE OF THE WEEK

If you want an opportunity to put into practice the truths you've learned in this lesson, complete one of the following challenges. Be ready to share the results of your challenge with your group.

1. **TAKE A SOCIAL MEDIA BREAK.** If you find yourself struggling with contentment when you view social media, take a break and shut off the screen. Make a commitment to not look at any social media for one week. See if this helps your contentment increase.

2. **HELP THOSE IN NEED.** Earlier in this lesson, on page 146, you wrote down the names of individuals or groups of fellow believers who are experiencing either financial, physical, or emotional needs. Choose one of these individuals or groups to help this week. Make a financial donation to one of the groups. Mail an anonymous money order to someone in need. Help meet physical needs by working around someone's yard or in their home. You'll be following the example of the Philippians who gave tangible help to Paul.

3. **QUIT COMPARING, START LEARNING.** When it comes to discontentment, how about we turn the tide? This week, when you are tempted to compare or want to weasel out of your life's circumstances, don't. Quit struggling to change the circumstances. Instead, ask yourself a few questions like:

   What does God want me to learn about Him that I might never discover if He were to suddenly pluck me out of this situation?

   What Christlike character traits is He trying to grow in me—patience, trust, compassion, faith?

Remember what author Elisabeth Elliot declared: "The secret is Christ in me, not me in a different set of circumstances."[3] Make this statement your motto this week.

MEMORY VERSE

OPTIONAL MEMORY VERSE

Remember that for each lesson, there is an optional memory verse provided to further internalize the message of the passages we've studied together. To assist you in this endeavor, all six passages are printed in the back of the study guide.

You may want to see if someone else in your group would like to come early or stay a few minutes after your group time so the two of you can practice saying the verses out loud to each other.

This session's verse is a bit long, but it's oh-so-crucial to remember and live by!

I have learned to be content in whatever circumstances I find myself. I know both how to make do with little, and I know how to make do with a lot. In any and all circumstances I have learned the secret of being content—whether well fed or hungry, whether in abundance or in need. I am able to do all things through him who strengthens me.

PHILIPPIANS 4:11b-13

I have learned to be content in whatever circumstances I find myself. I know both how to make do with little, and I know how to make do with a lot. In any and all circumstances I have learned the secret of being content—whether well fed or hungry, whether in abundance or in need. I am able to do all things through him who strengthens me.

PHILIPPIANS 4:11b-13

WEEK 7

WHAT MATTERS MOST

PARTNERSHIP IN THE GOSPEL

I give thanks to my God for every remembrance of you, always praying with joy for all of you in my every prayer, because of your partnership in the gospel from the first day until now.

PHILIPPIANS 1:3-5

VIEWER GUIDE

FAVORITE QUOTES

STAND-OUT SCRIPTURES

Video teaching sessions available for purchase at *LifeWay.com/WhatMattersMost*

GROUP GUIDE

ICEBREAKER

Have you ever encountered the story of a believer behind bars—a Christian who was incarcerated? This could be either someone you knew personally or one you read or heard about. What was their story? Were they able to discover joy despite their imprisonment? Explain.

1. *What stood out to you about Anthony's experience in prison?*

2. *Discuss the following statement that Anthony shared with Karen:* A lone sheep is nothing more than dinner. *What does this say about the importance of fellowship with other Christians?*

3. *While we may not be in a physical prison, sometimes we find ourselves imprisoned by one or more of the topics that Paul discussed in his letter to the church at Philippi. Have you ever felt trapped by any of the following:*

   - The opinions of others
   - Relationship conflicts
   - Sickness
   - Enemies
   - Suffering—either physical or emotional
   - Feeling bound by your past
   - Experiencing pressure in the present
   - Fear of the future
   - Worry over someone or something
   - Wrong thinking
   - Comparison
   - Regret for sinful choices

   How has this Bible study helped you find freedom from these traps?

4. *How has digging into the Letter of Philippians helped you in your walk with God? Which week of personal study especially spoke to you? In what ways?*

5. *Take a few moments to glance over your notes from the seven video teaching sessions. What truths jump out at you? What did you learn that you want to remember in the future?*

6. *We discovered Philippians has much to say about two aspects of life we encounter daily—relationships and circumstances. What have you learned about either of these subjects? Is there a particular verse that speaks specifically to the one you chose?*

7. *How would you sum up the main message of Paul's letter to the Philippians in just a sentence or two?*

ON YOUR OWN

What is one change God desires for you to make in your life, based upon something you have learned in this study? Write a brief prayer that declares that change, asking God to give you the boldness and power to make it. After several minutes, allow participants to share with the group the results of their *On Your Own* time.

PRAYER TIME

Take turns praying about the lessons from this study of Philippians. Designate one person—perhaps the group facilitator—to close out the prayer time.

LEADER GUIDE

It thrills my soul that you have chosen to facilitate a group study of *What Matters Most: A Study of Philippians*. Thank you in advance for your time, work, prayers, and presence as you lead the women in your group. This study takes a deep look into this important letter from the apostle Paul to his friends in the church of Philippi. It is chock-full of important doctrines of the faith and practical ways to live them out. It serves as a manual for the Christian on what to think and how to live.

In order to insure you are well prepared and have the best experience possible, here is some helpful information for you:

1. **VIDEO TEACHING.** The videos are available in the leader kit (item number 005802633) as well as by download (you can rent or buy the videos) at *LifeWay.com/WhatMattersMost*. These teaching videos are strongly recommended to be used as part of the study.

2. **GET THE WORD OUT.** Be sure to advertise this study early and utilize all methods for getting the word out. Post it on your church's website, send emails to potential attendees, and promote it on all forms of social media. It is best to start advertising the study four to six weeks before it begins. The study requires seven sessions to complete. Visit *LifeWay.com/WhatMattersMost* for free promotional materials to help get the word out about your upcoming study.

3. **SCHEDULE.** Each individual session will require sixty to seventy-five minutes. Be sure to start promptly in order to honor everyone's time. In your group time, you will view the teaching video together, then lead a group discussion using the questions provided in the Group Guide that accompanies each Viewer Guide. You'll close with a time of personal reflection and prayer

4. **STAY IN TOUCH.** Prepare a sign-up sheet with space for names, email addresses, and phone numbers. If you desire, make copies for everyone in the group during the session so they can be in touch between meeting times.

5. **GET COZY.** Make an effort to create a comfortable environment for the meetings. Arrange seating in a circle during discussion time. Make sure each participant understands that whatever is shared in the group will remain confidential. If your group is

large (ten or more women), you may want to watch the video teaching together, and then split into smaller groups for the discussion time. If you do split into smaller groups, make sure to enlist other volunteers to facilitate the small group discussions. If you would like to offer a light snack to your group, feel free to do so. Just make sure you allow for this on the schedule.

6. **CHILDCARE.** If your group will need childcare, be sure to organize this early to ensure there are enough workers to watch the children.

7. **BIBLE STUDY BOOKS.** Each participant will need a Bible study book. You can handle obtaining these books in one of two ways. Either direct each participant to purchase and obtain the book on their own, or you (or someone else) purchase all the books needed. If you choose the latter, make sure you do a pre-study sign-up so you have a good idea of the number of books needed. Distribute the books and collect payment at your first group meeting. If you will be ordering the books, check to see how long the books will take to arrive so you are assured they will be there by the first meeting. For those who want to attend the study but are not financially able to purchase a book, make scholarships available to them.

8. **EARLY PREP.** Secure a DVD player and TV for each session and make sure it is placed in the room before your meeting begins. Make sure to watch the video before your group meets. Take note of anything you want to highlight from the video teaching. Also, look over the discussion questions so you are prepared to facilitate the interactive time of the session. If you're going to have more than one group for the discussion time, encourage your small group leaders to prepare well.

9. **PERSONAL STUDY.** Note that between the sessions there is personal study to complete. This work can be done over three to five days at the pace each participant desires. There are not regimented days of study, but rather the material is presented in a natural flow. Each personal study section begins with a *Read It Carefully* section designed to allow the participant to slowly pore over the verses. Next is a *Study It Prayerfully* section where the women dive into a deeper analysis of the Scriptures. They are given historical background and meanings from the original Greek language in which this letter was written. Finally, there is a *Live It Out Practically* section where members are issued two to three challenges for the week and encouraged to pick one to complete. The challenges provide an opportunity for participants to live out the truths they have learned, weaving them naturally into their everyday lives.

10. **PRAYER.** Most importantly, be sure to pray daily for the women who attend the study. And pray for yourself as you prepare to lead throughout the duration of your time together. Ask God to draw the women closer to Him and teach them the lessons He has for them from Philippians.

11. **AGENDA.** Finally, here is a possible study agenda with suggested time frames. If you are also providing refreshments, you may do so at the beginning or the close of the class.

    1. Welcome and record info on the class's sign-up sheet. (5 minutes)
    2. Watch the video together as a large group. (25-30 minutes)
    3. Discuss the video teaching using the questions provided in the Bible study books. (25-35 minutes)
       Discussion set up:
       - Icebreaker question (3 minutes)
       - 6-8 questions for group discussion (15-25 minutes)
       - On Your Own reflection question done quietly and individually (5 minutes)
       - Prayer time as a group (2 minutes)
    4. Closing thoughts (2-5 minutes)

May God bless you as you facilitate this study. It is our deepest desire that together your group learns *what matters most*—knowing and serving Jesus Christ.

ENDNOTES

WEEK 1

1. Charles R. Erdman, *The Epistle of Paul to the Philippians* (Philadelphia: The Westminster Press, 1932).
2. Bob Dylan. "Gotta Serve Somebody." Recorded 1979 Track 1 on *Slow Train Coming.* Columbia. Compact Disc.
3. C. S. Lewis, *Letters of C.S. Lewis* (Orlando: Houghton Mifflin Harcourt Publishing Company, 1966), 363.

WEEK 2

1. William Barclay, *The Letters to the Philippians, Colossians, and Thessalonians* (Louisville, KY: Westminster Knox Press, 1975), 30.
2. G. K. Chesterton with Michael W. Perry, *Chesterton Day by Day: The Wit and Wisdom of G. K. Chesterton* (Seattle: Inkling Books, 2002).
3. "Definition of Preposition" *Quizlet.com.* Accessed on February 26, 2018, https://quizlet.com/104905331/com-101-second-test-flash-cards/.

WEEK 3

1. "Definition of phroneō" (accent over the o) *Bible Hub* http://biblehub.com/greek/5426.htm.
2. Ibid.
3. William Law, *A Practical Treatise Upon Christian Perfection* (London: G. Robinson, 1783), 193.
4. Ibid, Barclay, 48-49.
5. Ibid, Barclay, 49-50.
6. Ibid, Barclay, 57.

WEEK 4

1. Gail Herman, *Who Is Wayne Gretzky?* (New York: Grosset & Dunlap, 2015), 21.
2. John Mason, *Know Your Limits – Then Ignore Them* (Tulsa, OK: Insight Publishing Group, 1999), 123.
3. Henry David Thoreau, "16 of History's Greatest Philosophers Reveal the Secret to Happiness" *Business Insider, India.* Accessed on February 26, 2018, https://www.businessinsider.in/16-of-historys-greatest-philosophers-reveal-the-secret-to-happiness/Happiness-is-like-a-butterfly-the-more-you-chase-it-the-more-it-will-elude-you-but-if-you-turn-your-attention-to-other-things-it-will-come-and-sit-softly-on-your-shoulder-Henry-David-Thoreau-born-in-1817-in-Massachusetts-/slideshow/54902803.cms.
4. Mark Twain, *The Wit and Wisdom of Mark Twain: A Book of Quotations* (Mineola, New York: Dover Publications, 1999), 19.
5. Lindsay Lowe, "'Happiness is a Warm Puppy': 10 Peanuts Quotes to Make You Smile" *Parade* Posted November 25, 2017; accessed February 26, 2018. https://parade.com/623152/lindsaylowe/happiness-is-a-warm-puppy-10-peanuts-quotes-to-make-you-smile/.
6. J. R. R. Tolkien, *The Hobbit* (New York: Del Rey Books, 1937), 69.

WEEK 5

1. Debbie McDaniel, "40 Powerful Quotes from Corrie Ten Boom" *Crosswalk.com.* Published May 21, 2015; accessed February 26, 2018, https://www.crosswalk.com/faith/spiritual-life/inspiring-quotes/40-powerful-quotes-from-corrie-ten-boom.html.

WEEK 6

1. Debbie McDaniel, "40 Inspiring Quotes from Elisabeth Elliot" *Crosswalk.com.* Published June 17, 2015; accessed February 26, 2018, https://www.crosswalk.com/faith/spiritual-life/inspiring-quotes/40-inspiring-quotes-from-elisabeth-elliot.html.
2. Ibid.
3. Ibid.

Now I want you to know, brothers and sisters, that what has happened to me has actually advanced the gospel.

PHILIPPIANS 1:12

Just one thing: As citizens of heaven, live your life worthy of the gospel of Christ.

PHILIPPIANS 1:27a

Brothers and sisters, I do not
consider myself to have taken hold
of it. But one thing I do: Forgetting
what is behind and reaching
forward to what is ahead, I pursue
as my goal the prize promised by
God's heavenly call in Christ Jesus.

PHILIPPIANS 3:13-14

Don't worry about anything, but
in everything, through prayer and
petition with thanksgiving, present
your requests to God. And the
peace of God, which surpasses
all understanding, will guard your
hearts and minds in Christ Jesus.
PHILIPPIANS 4:6-7

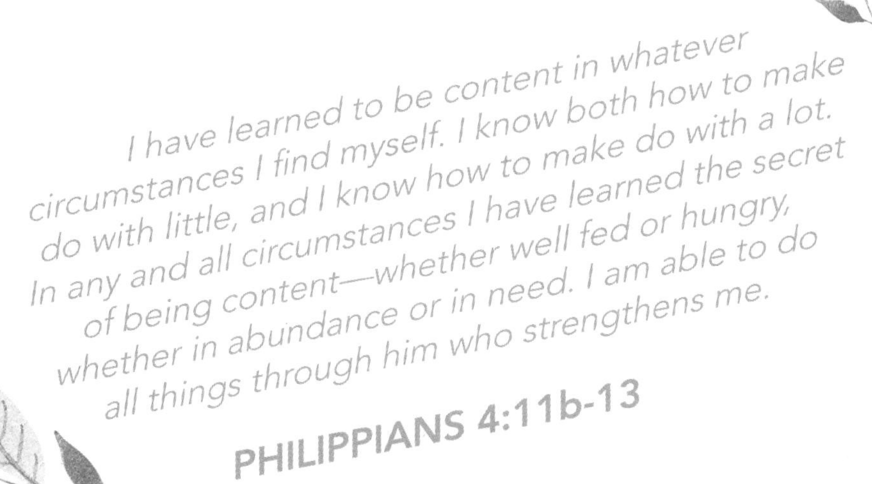
I have learned to be content in whatever
circumstances I find myself. I know both how to make
do with little, and I know how to make do with a lot.
In any and all circumstances I have learned the secret
of being content—whether well fed or hungry,
whether in abundance or in need. I am able to do
all things through him who strengthens me.
PHILIPPIANS 4:11b-13

Additional Studies from Proverbs 31 Authors

FINDING I AM

By Lysa TerKeurst
6 Sessions

Explore the I AM statements of Jesus found in the Gospel of John. Learn to trade feelings of emptiness and depletion for the fullness of knowing who Jesus is in this interactive, in-depth Bible study.

Bible Study Book	005784578	*$14.99*
Leader Kit	005784579	*$99.99*

LifeWay.com/FindingIAM

RACHEL & LEAH

By Nicki Koziarz
6 Sessions

Arm yourself with biblical truths to combat comparison by studying the account of Rachel and Leah. Learn to be content without becoming complacent, and discover godly wisdom to quiet the incessant *Why her?* question in your head. Develop greater awareness of your insecurities, and learn to stop the lies in their tracks.

Bible Study Book 005794724 *$12.99*

LifeWay.com/RachelAndLeah

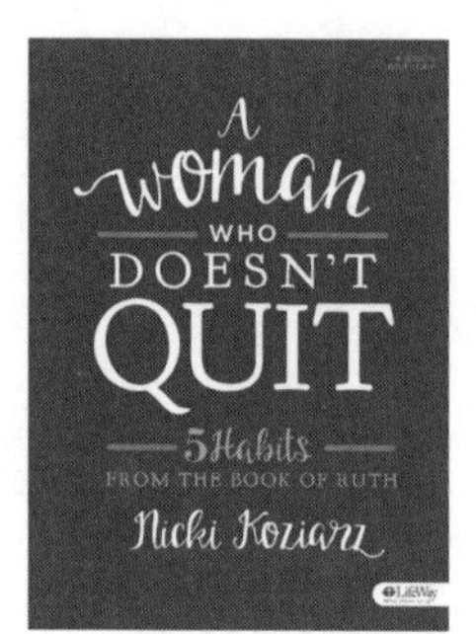

A WOMAN WHO DOESN'T QUIT

By Nicki Koziarz
6 Sessions

Walk through the Book of Ruth, looking to the Moabite woman for five practical habits that kept her from quitting and kept her eyes focused on God. Because a woman who refuses to quit influences her world in ways she could never have imagined.

Bible Study Book 005772638 *$12.99*

LifeWay.com/5HabitsStudy

800.458.2772 | LifeWay Christian Stores

LifeWay | Women

Pricing and availability subject to change without notice.